MW01194539

To: Geri
I hope you will enjoy
my Book.

Donna

LUKE 8:48
A SUPERNATURAL
JOURNEY
of
FAITH

DONNA DAVENPORT COX

BALBOA.
PRESS
A DIVISION OF HAY HOUSE

Balboa Press books may be ordered through booksellers or by contacting:

Balboa Press
A Division of Hay House
1663 Liberty Drive
Bloomington, IN 47403
www.balboapress.com
1 (877) 407-4847

Because of the dynamic nature of the Internet, any web addresses or links contained in this book may have changed since publication and may no longer be valid. The views expressed in this work are solely those of the author and do not necessarily reflect the views of the publisher, and the publisher hereby disclaims any responsibility for them.

The author of this book does not dispense medical advice or prescribe the use of any technique as a form of treatment for physical, emotional, or medical problems without the advice of a physician, either directly or indirectly. The intent of the author is only to offer information of a general nature to help you in your quest for emotional and spiritual well-being. In the event you use any of the information in this book for yourself, which is your constitutional right, the author and the publisher assume no responsibility for your actions.

Any people depicted in stock imagery provided by Thinkstock are models, and such images are being used for illustrative purposes only.
Certain stock imagery © Thinkstock.

Print information available on the last page.

ISBN: 978-1-5043-6564-2 (sc)
ISBN: 978-1-5043-6595-6 (hc)
ISBN: 978-1-5043-6565-9 (e)

Library of Congress Control Number: 2016914649

Balboa Press rev. date: 09/19/2016

Author's Page

Welcome, and thank you so much for choosing to read my book; I'm humbled you chose mine. For those of you who don't know me personally, I'm as southern as a gal gets. I talk southern, cook with a southern twist, and treat everyone with Southern Hospitality. So I guess it's only fitting I write southern too.

I was born and raised in the small town of Williamston, SC where I still live today among some of the nicest, most kind and caring folks you'll ever meet. It's a great old historic town where most of us know and even like each other- except for a few old soreheads. I bless people's hearts about a million times a day and give out hugs like there's no tomorrow. When life throws me a basket of Lemons, I just toss 'em in my big old glass of sweet tea and move right along.

Now you may notice from time to time in my writings, I'll flip flop a bit on occasion. One minute I'm liable to be in past tense, the next present tense or future and it may be all in the same paragraph. You may find me in first person, second or third, all the way up to a person you've never heard of before. What I'm trying to say is, I write how I talk and I can promise you that every word, absolutely and without any doubt, comes from the heart.

You may even notice at times I seem a little long winded with a sentence. That's because I love to explain by stretching it out. For me it just flows better, especially if I use the word "that" and throw in a few extra commas. It's just my style of writing, so I hope you'll understand.

con't

Years ago, I did complete writing school which gave me a great starting foundation. I've had articles published in The Old Schoolhouse Magazine and Homeschool Enrichment Magazine as well. I enjoy my Facebook advice page, The Sage Grinder, and love doing Angel card readings for family and friends. I've had extensive studies in Herbal Medicine and Plant Use, Irish Folk Medicine, Candle Therapy, Crystal Healing Therapy, Appalachian Folk Medicine, and eight years of Native American Healing practices while studying with one of the greatest shamans to ever walk this great land.

To say my studies are ongoing is definitely an understatement, for I just love to learn. I wish for every one of you, all the joys of life. I hope you'll be blessed by reading my book, as much as I've been by writing it.

Love You,
Donna

Donna Davenport Cox
may be contacted by email at:
ddcox63@gmail.com

Dedication

To my wonderful husband Guerry: *You've seen me at my best as well as my worst; I'm so grateful to have you. I'm thankful for all you do for me and for your continued love and support. Thank you for reading and re- reading my chapters so many times your eyes probably hurt. Without you, this book would not have been possible.*

To our Children (Ashley, Dusty, Halston, Cale, Kayla, Leigh Ann, Michael, and Lauren): *I'm so very blessed to have all of you in our lives. Thank you for putting up with me, especially my OCD. I'm so proud of the men and women you've become. Each of you inspires me in your own way to be a better person.*

To Our Grandchildren who we adore (Logan, Luke, Khloe, Bristol, and Eva): *What can I possibly say about those who bring so much joy into our lives? I love you all dearly and look so forward to watching each of you grow and learn about the blessings of life.*

To our dear friends (Leah, Sue, and Roman): *Thank you for your continued encouragement, even when I've felt like giving up. You're all very special to me and I thank God each and every day for you.*

To my Cousin Linda: *Growing up you were always the big sister I never had. When Mama passed, you became my second Mama. I appreciate the many times you've been there for me and helped when no one else could. Thank you for always encouraging me to do what I need to do. I love you with all my heart.*

To my Lifelong Best Friend Jennifer: I honestly don't have enough words to express how I feel about our friendship. We've sailed many rough waters, as well as smooth ones. You've watched my children grow up and my parents pass away. If I had this same lifetime to live again, I'd want you right by my side. Thank you for all you do for me; I love you dearly.

To Daddy, Mama, and my Mother in Law Jan: Thank you for inspiring me to write this book through events in your life. I appreciate all of your help from the Other Side. I miss you all so much but know I will see you again soon.

To Rachel and all the Guides: Thank you for helping me along this path on my journey and for your guidance and insight.

To Red Cloud: This book would never have been written without you. You've been my guide and inspiration for many years now. You not only taught me about life, but you've taught me how to live. You've shown me the ways of the Universe and encouraged me when I've been down and lost. I'm blessed beyond measure to know and love you, and blessed to call you my friend.

If you understand the journey the walk is a lot easier.

It's a natural instinct to be afraid of dying. It shouldn't be, it's the greatest act in the world.

Luke 8:48 "A Supernatural Journey of Faith"

Contents

Chapter One

The Angel Visit

Turning five was such a peak year for me. I really don't remember a birthday party, Christmas, or any special occasion that year, although I know the events took place. Those memories just failed to store themselves in my brain I guess. One profound recollection engrained in my head, was almost losing my Dad; then again, it's not every day you meet your guardian angel either. My world, from as far back as I can remember, seemed to always gravitate around the supernatural. Many times my mind has wandered back to those early years and how life just always somehow equipped me for challenges I would face; ones not only in childhood, but my adult years also.

In May of 1969, Daddy had battled seven kidney stones in less than six months. The pain and suffering he endured at times was almost unbearable, not to mention how hard it was on Mama. I never realized, until I was older, what a strong lady my Mama was. It was an appreciation I could not fully grasp, until many years of seasoning on my part had gone by. One day, the thought of how she must have been a saint hit me like a bolt of lightning. I'm sure it wasn't easy dealing with ongoing health problems week after week.

Mama worked hard at her full time job. She also ran several businesses on the side for years, just to help pay Daddy's medical bills. It was a time when people stuck together through thick and thin; a time when you did what you had to do to survive. I've been told more than once I come from good stock; somehow knowing that makes me feel very blessed. My fortune lies in my education of life skills from those around me like my Parents and Grandparents. If you ask me to list three core traits among all of them, it would be love, dedication, and humbleness. I'd like to think I inherited at least a couple.

When I have a conversation with someone about daddy and the numerous stones he had, they just frown in disbelief. To date I've had eleven of those little Demons myself, but over a ten year span. I know the pain I've felt, so I can't imagine the effects on body and mind in dealing with it on a regular basis.

Not a week went by, for several years, without a doctor's visit or two for injections to relieve the pain. Many times Mama woke me up during the night to put my shoes on and get in the car so Daddy could see the doctor for kidney colic; that's what they called it. In addition to experiencing them myself, I've lived the torment through his eyes many times. I've seen those tiny little stones bring Daddy to his knees; the only relief being a shot of pain medication.

After almost two years of regular visits to the same doctor, we discovered him to be extremely kind and caring. He told Mama, during one of those times, that although he didn't make house calls, he was always available after hours. That was the beginning of us going directly to his house for Daddy's treatments. Instead of waiting in the ER, Daddy would call the doctor's home phone, no matter what time it was at night. If he was home, the doctor would be standing in his doorway as we pulled in the drive. Daddy would get his shot, pay him cash, and we'd be on our way in less than two minutes. After that, we'd come home and try to finish out the night's sleep as best we could; if there was any night left.

The medicine usually lasted for a few days, depending on the size of the stone. Many times there was more than one. I've had people ask why he never had the lithotripsy to break them up. They did consider it at one point. His doctors felt it would do more harm than good due to the amount and kind of stones his kidney produced.

Though Daddy was born with three kidneys, something was wrong from the beginning with one. The oddity of being born with more than two kidneys does happen, and normally it's not dangerous. My Parents were told on rare occasions they do begin, after a few years, to give problems. In Daddy's situation, the extra one was smaller. It sat on top of one of the other two, but didn't function at all. One doctor even entertained the idea he may have been a twin but none of the various medical theories offered were ever proven.

Daddy's daily health issues would have bought most people a one way ticket to the hospital. For us, it was a regular routine we'd become accustomed to. Mama told us his real problems started shortly after their marriage. By the time I was six years old he'd been hospitalized, or visited the ER, over 40 times. He always worked a full-time job, never complained, and did the best he could; we took life one day at a time. We never made any long term plans for traveling. We never knew if Daddy would be able to make the trip. I often labeled him throughout life as being the strongest man I knew. I failed miserably to give Mama the credit she deserved in holding the Strongest Woman title.

Daddy had every test known to modern science. Many times we traveled to the Baptist hospital in Winston -Salem, North Carolina; Emory in Atlanta, Georgia; and Duke University in Durham, North Carolina. One specialist after another felt confident he could get to the root cause of the stones and bleeding. Each trip and many tests later left each one shaking their heads, baffled as to why it continued. Daddy was put on every diet you could think of. He was given hundreds of different medications to try, many being experimental drugs; nothing helped and nothing changed. One surgeon even told us it was a miracle he was still alive after everything he'd endured. The damage to his poor body through the years, had already taken its toll.

One Saturday afternoon, Daddy came in from working the garden early. He took a bath and got his suit clothes out for church the next day. It was a routine in our family to have everything laid out and ready to go. The Saturday before Mother's Day was always spent getting ready for the big event at our church; all special occasions were like that. Folks would plan all week for these fun filled times leading to finishing touches the day before.

Daddy had looked extremely pale all day. I'd have to say that most of the time he never let being sick stop him from getting his work done. At four in the afternoon, he already had pajamas on sitting bedside reading his Bible; it was something he did every night before going to sleep. I don't think there was even one time he did it because he felt he had too. It was like he couldn't wait to finish his daily routine, so he could read those sacred verses he'd come to love and depend on. I still recall his obituary where I included he'd read his Bible through in its entirety thirty two times. Daddy was never a proud man, never boastful, but he was proud of accomplishing that feat. In my eyes, it was always an admirable endeavor.

I climbed up beside Daddy and asked if he wanted to play a game of checkers. He smiled and patted me on the head like he usually did, telling me we'd play another day. That was the first time I noticed the underlined Bible verse in red. I could read pretty well by that age, so I read it to myself. Luke 8:48 "**And he said unto her, daughter, be of good comfort: thy faith hath made thee whole; go in peace**." I asked Daddy if he underlined that verse because of being so sick all the time. He closed his Bible and gave me the sweetest smile. "All God asks of us is to have faith and believe in Him. Your Mama gave me this Bible the first year we were married. I underlined this verse to show God that even though I have kidney problems, I know beyond the shadow of a doubt that someday I'll be healed." "But what if

God doesn't heal you?" I asked. Daddy said he knew He would in His own time.

Those early years were definitely the basis, or grounding I like to call it, for my path in life. They set the pace for the way I've always perceived and treated others. I raised my children with this grounding. I notice now, many times how it's been passed along to my Grandchildren. Their personalities are all so different but have one common thread; they all have a loving and kind heart. It really is just following the Golden Rule in our treatment of others.

Mama said Daddy needed some peace and quiet because he'd had a rough week working at the mill; the heat was terrible. Daddy said summer was coming on fast. Sometimes in the really hot months it got well over a hundred degrees in there, even with the industrial fans running. It definitely wasn't the easiest job in the world for someone with his type of health problems. Daddy was good at what he did and enjoyed his work. He took great pride in the machines he serviced and considered most of the folks he worked with to be family.

I recall many days when he got sick at work and had to leave. He was blessed beyond measure, throughout his career, to have great bosses who let him work around his normal schedule. Yes, there were days he left early but he always made the hours up. On good days, many times he would get up and head into work during the middle of the night. I think God just always put the right people in his life to help him. In return, they got a faithful worker who would go above and beyond to do his job right, always treating his coworkers with respect.

Many times before bed, Mama would check on Daddy to make sure he was okay. She would peek in, stand there for a few seconds, and watch to make sure his chest was moving. I can remember her rubbing cooking oil on the hinges so the door wouldn't squeak. Once Mama saw he was breathing, she sighed with relief that he was alright. I still recall those extra thick gold and brown floral curtains hanging in their bedroom to block the sunlight out. Those curtains must have hung there for twenty five years or more.

If Mama wasn't home, the responsibility for keeping an eye on Daddy fell on me; many times I called her if he got sick. When he felt extremely bad, he would finish up his work, cook supper (which he loved to do), and be in bed before she ever got home. All of the above was done only after getting his outside chores done first. Daddy would say, "Just because a person feels bad it don't mean the work stops." He would often times lock the door and tell me to watch television till Mama got home. "You stay put and don't go outside," he would say; I kept a close watch on him always. I really loved him and felt so much sadness for the daily pain he endured.

That same night, I woke to Mama screaming, it was 3 A.M. I knew this because Daddy bought me a Charlie Brown clock with Snoopy lying on the dog house. I loved that clock and checked the lighted face every time I woke up. I could hear Mama calling the rescue squad, telling them they needed to come to our house. I looked in on Daddy; he looked kind of bluish in color, I couldn't see him breathing. I'd seen this before but never as bad; he wasn't moving at all. I developed that gut feeling of something terrible happening when I was so young. That was definitely, one of those times. Little did I know, that feeling would remain with me my whole life; it would emerge at times I least expected it. After my near death experience, it would magnify itself at times to the point it would make me physically sick.

Mama told me to put my clothes and shoes on that we'd be leaving. The rescue squad was only about 2 ½ miles from our house. They were used to getting calls from us at all hours. Many times I feel Daddy's life was saved because of their quick response. In all honesty, they became like family to us. Mama always took comfort in the fact that when she called, they would get there in minutes.

My stomach was in knots as I unlocked the door. I always got a sick feeling but this time it was worse; I prayed hard that Daddy would be okay. As I type these words, those overwhelming feelings once again return, even after all these years.

The Rescue Squad arrived, worked with him a few minutes, and told us he had a faint pulse. As they lifted him off the bed onto the stretcher, I saw that he was lying in a puddle of blood. I guess most children would have been scared to death but I was used to this type of situation. I'd seen puddles of blood many times. It never got any easier, even as the years and many experiences passed by. It didn't take long as a child to become accustomed to it.

Just before loading Daddy into the ambulance, my Mama's brother Buddy drove up. He passed our house going home and happened to see the lights. He drove Mama and me to the hospital; the two of them hardly said a word the whole way there. Looking back, I see now that Mama probably felt daddy wasn't going to make it. She explained to Buddy what had happened, then sat silently staring out the window the rest of the way there. Buddy always did love Daddy; they treated each other like brothers with a bond that would last sixty years.

Buddy dropped us off at the emergency room entrance so he could park the car. Mama sat me down in front of the nurse's desk; she told me to stay there while she checked in. I was used to the routine, for I'd done it many times before. I always carried my baby doll with me, along with my bag of coloring books, sticker books, and crayons; many times it was a long night or all night. I often wondered why Mama didn't send me to my Grandparent's house very much, but she didn't. Looking back on it now, her reasoning was probably that we went to the hospital so often she just couldn't think of anything but getting Daddy the help he needed.

The nurses immediately took Daddy back and the wait began. After a while, the Doctor came out and told Mama they were running more tests. He appeared to be in Acute Kidney Failure. He said he was so sorry but it didn't look good for him because of his many health problems. His body appeared to be so broken down and weak from loss of blood. I distinctly remember his words, "the odds he'll recover are stacked against him." He told Mama it would probably be a good time to call the rest of the family and let them know.

Mama went to pieces as she followed the Doctor to Daddy's room. Buddy said he would go home to get the family and let everybody know what was going on. Any other time, I would have jumped at the chance to go with him because we always had fun. But this time was different, I felt so sick I just wanted to sit there. I had such a weight on my shoulders, like my body was a big blob of glue stuck to the chair; my head and heart hurt as well. I wanted desperately to cry but didn't want the nurse or anyone else to see me. I wanted to run and hide till the nightmare was over. I'd learned to be strong even at that young age. Throughout my life, that skill has served me well.

I held my doll tight. I talked to her like she was a real person. Many nights her comfort was all that kept me sane; she'd become a constant companion. Besides my best friend Jennifer, I was pretty much a loner so just a hug brought me great contentment. I stared at the picture I'd colored for Daddy. I wondered if I'd ever be able to give it to him or if I'd place it in his casket. I thought about the way he always prayed about everything. He would say, "If you have something on your mind, pray about it. Just talk to God like He's right there with you."

I began to pray and thank God for Daddy, Mama, my baby doll, and my little dachshund Bitsy. Daddy always said we should give thanks for our many blessings first, before asking for anything. I told God what a good man Daddy was and how he'd been real sick for a long time but he'd helped lots of people. I explained he was a deacon. We always went to church even when he was sick; I told God how much Daddy loved Mama and me. Tears flowed as I pointed out how Daddy always cut the grass, worked the garden, and tended to the animals. I said we needed him because Mama just didn't know how to do any of that stuff. Somehow, I knew God could understand that, being a Daddy himself. He had a lot to do every day with all the people in the world but I just knew he was listening. I was careful not to leave one little detail out. I had to cover every point in my petition so that He would know just how special Daddy was.

I can still remember the emergency room, how I sat in that chair in front of the desk like it was yesterday; the sterile smell still lingers in my mind. Many times I've made a visit to someone sick and found myself daydreaming of those years. Back then, children really weren't allowed in the hospital but we'd come to know a lot of the staff that worked there. I guess that made it easier for Mama to take me with her.

Just as I said Amen, I felt someone touch my hand. I opened my eyes to see a lady sitting there next to me. She had white fluffy hair like my Grandmother, a sweet smile, and the most beautiful blue eyes I'd ever seen; the blue in her eyes was like no other color. Many times I've described them as being as blue as the Mediterranean Sea. It was as if she could see right through me down to my soul. I wasn't afraid, not in the least. She knew me somehow, and with that knowing came a great comfort that washed all over me. Mama had always taught me not to talk to strangers. In my heart I knew she was far from being that.

She patted my hand and her smile could have lit the whole room. The nurse sitting at the front desk kept busy doing whatever she was doing. I don't think she saw her; looking back on it now, I'm sure she didn't. Almost at the exact moment I felt her hand on mine, the nurse yelled for someone to check out the phone because it had gone dead. I remember what a unique feeling I got from her. It was strange to me then; I really didn't know how to describe it as a child. In past years, I've felt that same feeling on many occasions. It was almost like a light electrical charge washed all over me; it made my body tingle. That feeling stayed with me for several hours after she'd gone.

The lady with the blue eyes told me God had heard my sweet prayers for Daddy. She said that the love between a parent and a child can be one of the greatest loves in the Universe. She suggested I stop worrying because everything would be alright. She said that all of our prayers are heard, not one goes unheard by God and the angels. "There are special angels who do nothing but deal with the many prayers that are prayed every day," she said. "Your Daddy can choose tonight to go home with me if he wishes. God will also let him stay if he wants to because he still has business to finish."

I knew when she spoke, she was an angel. Actually, I knew it when I saw her eyes and her smile; she was so gentle when she touched my hand. I asked if she was our Guardian Angel because Daddy always said everybody has one and I wanted to know. She grinned and said, "Let's just say I've known you since before you were ever born. I know everything about you and your family. I've always been here and always will be here to help take care of you; all you need do is ask." Then she told me yes, that everyone does have their very own Guardian Angel and some people have more than one, depending on how hard they make their life here.

I really didn't understand some of what she was saying at the time, but I still remember the comfort of her words and the sound of her voice. I told her I bet the angels have a hard time keeping up with everybody; she laughed and said that sometimes it can be most difficult. "We all have lessons we need to learn," she said. "Some learn faster than others and some never learn what they are supposed to, so they do it again and again."

She kissed me on the forehead, got up, and walked toward the door. She turned around and gave me a smile and a wink; I watched as she faded and disappeared. I wasn't afraid and the sickness I'd felt was gone because I knew Daddy would be alright. I knew that everything wrong on that night would somehow be okay; Daddy's life would be spared. I knew my prayers had been answered. From that moment on, I would pray for many people through the years and still do. It was one of many nights I would experience just how powerful prayer is. Forty years later, I would see and talk with her again. I learned that prayer and love are the most powerful forces in the universe.

Mama came out and sat beside me, she was so pitiful. Her eyes were red and swollen from where she'd cried. I hugged her and said not to worry, Daddy would be okay. She looked straight into my eyes; she told me how sick Daddy was. "I'm so sorry but he's just not going to make it." I told her again not to worry because an angel came down from Heaven and told me Daddy was going to be just fine. Mama smiled, I knew she didn't believe me but I knew what had happened. I didn't care if anyone believed me; it didn't matter as long as Daddy was okay.

Family began to pour in the waiting area; Papa came straight to me and scooped me up in his big old lap. He was always wearing his overalls and I loved all the little pockets on the bib. I felt so safe and secure with Papa and Nannie. I don't remember my other Grandparents much but Nannie and Papa were always there for me. I told them about the Angel's visit, how Daddy would be okay, and how I'd prayed for him. Nannie said we should always believe in the angels, for God sends them to help us in times of need. Papa sat and colored two pages with me that night while we waited for news.

My Mother's Parents always loved Daddy like their own son. He was good to them; many times he helped Papa or took him somewhere he needed to go. Daddy loved my Nannie like his own Mama. She would always call him when she made a pound cake or an old fashioned blackberry cobbler because that was his favorite. We saw them almost every day and in many ways, I felt more at home with them than at my own home. It was almost like getting lost in my own little world on their small farm among the trees and the animals.

After a while, the nurse announced there had been a change; "the Doctor will be right out," she said. Mama looked at Nannie and shook her head. My aunts and uncles were there along with our Preacher. They gathered around as the doctor came out. "Mrs. Davenport, I really don't know how to tell you this but Mr. Davenport is awake. He is asking for you and your daughter. I have no reason to believe he won't fully recover; it's nothing short of a miracle." I immediately lit up with a smile. It was the best news in the world, the news I'd been waiting to hear.

Everybody smiled and hugged each other. In less than an hour, Daddy was sitting up eating a sandwich the nurse had found for him; he'd told her he was starving. Daddy was released the next day. When we got home there was food everywhere. Neighbors brought in cakes, casseroles, pies, sandwiches, and any kind of food you could think of. I was so happy to have him back home. When I gave Daddy the picture I'd colored for him, he put it in his Bible. He told me he would keep it forever and he did. Many times through the years, I saw him take that picture out and smile as if he were reminiscing. In later years, even after he developed Alzheimer's, he still had the picture and knew where it came from.

Several days later, Daddy told our Preacher about a dream he'd had while in the hospital. He said his Grandpa came to visit and brought an angel with him, she was beautiful. She told him to be of good cheer, that his time on Earth was not yet complete unless he chose it to be. Great Grandpa had been gone a long time. There would be several times through the years that he would come to visit Daddy when he was sick; I always thought that was special.

Daddy said that Jesus walked with him. He told him how important it is not only to pray, but to believe in what we pray for; like it had already happened. He said if we believe enough in what we ask for, it will come to us unless God sees different. Jesus told Daddy that God only wants the best for us and we should always be helpful to each other, even when someone has wronged us. Daddy said Jesus explained to him that when we do for others or give to others, especially when we have nothing to give, that's when the blessings of life flow the most. When we do that, we're giving or doing out of pure faith and a loving heart.

Sometime after that, Daddy made a rock alter down behind the old church. He was faithful to go there and pray for our family and friends over sixty years; my boys have seen it many times. That was long ago now, but I've seen remnants of it. I've often stared at those rocks, thinking of the times Daddy would send up heartfelt prayers for those who needed them. Even more special, was the knowing that he really believed the miracles he prayed for would transpire one way or another.

At fifty-two years of age, I consider my life to be so blessed. Though my childhood was not normal as far as some of the other kids growing up around me, it shaped my life for a greater purpose. Yes I witnessed many miracles, many of which I will share with you throughout these pages. The only way I can possibly describe these miracles are through Supernatural Powers. That power is very real and when you've witnessed it firsthand, you know just how real it is.

My goal in writing this book is to show you that we all have a higher power we can depend on. It doesn't mean our lives will always be easy, for they won't. It means that even in the depths of our darkest despair, we have the knowing that we are loved. It's a knowing that we are cared for, by those precious heavenly beings that surround us on a daily basis; by the One who created us for a higher purpose.

Chapter Two

Prayer in Numbers

If I could spend all day counting the blessings in my life, that day would run into tomorrow, next week, and next year; let's not kid ourselves, it would be never ending. I've always been a big fan of the saying, "There is always, always something to be thankful for." I feel that even in the midst of hard times, thanks should be given in everything. One day my oldest Son and I were having a deep conversation about life in general. I listened intently as he quoted some pretty wise words to me, "If we don't go through some bad times, we'll never understand how great the good times really are." I've seen many days where I've faced some of my worst moments. But even in the pits of despair, this quote by Albert Clark stays close to my heart, "In daily life we must see that it is not happiness that makes us grateful, but gratefulness that makes us happy."

To say I've been blessed by the people in my life, and things I've experienced, is without question an understatement. Being older, more seasoned as I call it, I've come to appreciate even the smallest of life's trials and tribulations I'm constantly dealt. During those times you'll find the greatest blessings you've ever known. Take a moment and really study your life. Are you somewhat happy, satisfied, content, and healthy? If you can answer yes to just one of these success words, then count your blessings. When the trials and tribulations show up, just brush yourself off and keep on going; for that is when we advance the most and move forward.

Guerry and I lead a pretty simple life. We really don't differ that much in the happiness department. We enjoy our Kids and Grandchildren; spending what time we can with them is number one on our list. Add in a get together with friends to eat, a little antiquing, an occasional movie, or watching a couple of shows on Netflix, and we're all set.

Guerry likes reading, going to our local park and flea market, and keeping up with the girls (his chickens). He's also stepped right into Daddy's shoes as far as keeping a beautiful yard around the old home place. I've watched him take great pride in accomplishing that task through the years. For me, I love a clean house, cooking, making my salves and tinctures, continuing my herbal studies, working with my flowers, and sneaking in some writing.

I've learned in getting older I desire more of that simple life. When my Children were growing up, I was in one mode; it was always 24/7. Lord, I see this in my Children now; they're just in that hurried season of life. But for Guerry and me, we're learning to slow down a bit and just breathe. There's nothing more peaceful than sitting on one of the park benches, taking in our clean small town air, while watching the Grandchildren play. I've learned firsthand how important slowing down is in our technological world of today. Once you master the technique, you really get a grasp on the way life should be. You never crave the fast pace again. Matter of fact, when a busy, stressful day sneaks up on you, it does nothing but cause chaos and confusion; at least that's how it works for me.

For most of my adult life, I was so busy I never knew how to enjoy the simple things. I appreciated those blessings, but never stopped long enough to grasp them. It's different for me now, I'm in a new season and I adore it. I love that my Children are doing well; I love being Granmama. My heart delights in watching those little people grow into their own distinct personalities; that feeling is priceless. You grandparents know where I'm coming from. When I became a parent, I never prayed so hard in my life as I did for my Children. Now that I'm a grandparent, I pray even more for my Grandchildren. I've spent many sleepless nights talking to God over a situation involving family, as I'm sure most of you have as well.

Parts of my childhood were no different than kids I grew up with, except that most of my friends had siblings; I had none. Yep, I've experienced the old, "Oh you're an only child you must be spoiled rotten," label many times. I'll be the first to say that being an only child does have its disadvantages. My Parents waited a long time for me to come along, eight years after marriage. Daddy said he never gave up and cried the first time he held me. He thanked God for the blessings bestowed on him and Mama. He really thought he would never have the opportunity to be a dad.

Daddy said I was a good baby; he delighted in watching me grow and learn things. He told me once that he knew I was different or special because I preferred to be alone. Looking back on my life now, I can still see that trait in me. I can be a total social butterfly, never meeting a stranger as my Nannie would say. After the fun and hoopla though, I'm ready to climb back into my little world; I crave that alone time. It's like a required need to recharge my batteries. It may only be reading a book, or writing, or maybe a cup of coffee while checking emails or Facebook. My psyche just feels the need to embrace that solitude at least once per day to function at my best.

Nannie always said I had a heart for others. She knew that the day she heard me crying at four years old when I heard the song, "Away in a Manger." When she asked why the tears, I told her it was because I felt so bad for the Baby Jesus. He didn't have a warm comfortable bed to sleep in like I did when He was born. Nannie's favorite saying as I grew older was, "Child, you simply cannot save the world and take care of everyone, but somehow I know you're going to try." If I had a hundred dollar bill for every time she said that to me, I'd be monetarily rich as well. I couldn't help it. From a very young age I'd always been drawn to those who needed help or a shoulder to cry on.

Daddy and Mama worked so much that I was a constant staple at my Grandparents house; matter of fact, being home didn't even feel right to me. I have no doubt my Mama loved me dearly, but Daddy and I had a special bond. One that lasted until his mission here was complete and he returned home. Mama and I were never close during my childhood years; she was always involved in so many projects, we never had that chance. Eventually, we did form a bond a few years before her death and believe it or not, I actually miss her more each day. I think that feeling comes from having the opportunity to spend so much time with Daddy growing up and never the time I should've had with Mama. I feel in some ways, I missed out on a great opportunity to be her Daughter during those early years. I don't mind saying, I often feel robbed.

Mama was a good woman, a hard worker, and an excellent co-provider for our family. She was strong, "set in her ways," Daddy would say. I smile as I type these words because in many respects, I'm just like her and so is my Daughter as well. Guerry has remarked many times how strong the women in our family are, but we get the job done. Mama was one of those sun up to sun down working people. She took great delight in her accomplishments. I realize now because of her hard work and sacrifice, the path was paved for us to do the things we loved to do like fishing, hunting, searching for buried treasure, etc.

Life at our house was no easy road though, I assure you of that. I understand now at this stage in my life, why Mama felt she had to work as hard as she did. Looking back on when I was young, and at times stupid, I never appreciated the hours she put in or the sacrifices she made for us. Maybe that's why my heart aches so much for her now; I saw her as a workaholic. A mother who would rather be working her full time job, while catering weddings, anniversaries, showers, and parties on the side. She was a perfectionist alright; she didn't stop until every detail was right. The words, "I give up and I quit," just weren't in her vocabulary, nor are they in mine or my Children's.

Even though things were different with us and we never had that typical mother-daughter bond, I still always knew I was loved. Mama just wasn't one in her younger years to really show that love like Daddy did. Thankfully, by the time her Grandchildren came along, she was at the stage in life where she dedicated herself to them. I give her the award for being the very best top notch Grandmother my Children could've ever asked for. There's a lot to be said for the time in life when you become more seasoned. You learn to put aside things that don't matter as much, to make room for things that do. Although I'm still really busy at this point in my life, as I grow older I see myself beginning to do just that. I told my parents on many occasions, how grateful I was for everything they did for me and my Children in their younger years. Many times when they could have slowed down, they didn't because of being such selfless Grandparents.

Daddy's health problems began during a time when medical technology lacked the advances of today. Despite being born with major issues, his real problems started when he was in his twenties. When Daddy was in the army, he and his platoon were on maneuvers at Fort Rucker in Alabama. He was bitten one day by an Eastern Diamondback Rattlesnake in a foxhole. He remembered jumping in and feeling a sharp pain in his left forearm; he said he felt a fire like sensation rage through his entire body. After that, he never knew anything else until five days later when he woke up in the base hospital. His Commanding Officer said he was afraid they'd lost him. He said that snake was the biggest rattler he'd ever seen; it measured almost eight feet long and as big around as a baseball. Daddy wasn't fully released back to active duty for another two weeks after that. It was an event in his life he never fully recovered from but it would be later on before he realized that.

Daddy often talked of that experience, especially in his younger years. He said he remembered jumping into the foxhole and feeling pain and fire in his arm. He knew he passed out; when he woke up he was talking to his Great Grandfather. They were sitting on the creek bank fishing. His Great Grandfather told stories of when he was a boy growing up, the adventures he would take, and mischief he got into. He said times were hard back then because they didn't have a lot. They always had food and lots of love; that was all that mattered. Daddy said his Great Grandmother was there too. She hugged him and said to be of good courage for he would face many trials in his lifetime. She told of how God and the angels would always be there to see him through till his days here were over. She hugged him and said he would become an inspiration to many through the years.

Daddy said he wanted to stay in that peaceful place. He said the trees and flowers were beautiful; he felt good there. His Great Grandmother told him the snake bite would set the pace for health problems the rest of his life. She said it was meant to be but she would always be watching over him in everything he did. His Great Grandfather told him to always pray and pray earnestly, about anything that troubled him. He said, "Son, prayer is for everyone, just be specific about what you need." I actually have a small chalkboard hanging in my home with that very saying on it. Daddy's Great Grandparents had been gone for many years.

After returning home from the army, Daddy began to experience more kidney issues as well as stones. One infection was so bad he was hospitalized. He was told after tests were made he only had one kidney working. The other two were causing problems. The recommendation was made they be taken out as soon as possible. Back then, kidney surgery was much different than now; his scar looked like he'd been cut in half. The surgeon told Mama he felt sure the surgery would improve his health, but it didn't. For many years he battled severe kidney problems and infections; he suffered with having 312 kidney stones throughout his life.

It was after this major surgery, Daddy told of the angels being in the operating room. He specifically spoke about one angel in particular he said was as tall as the ceiling. He described everything in that room to Mama and said his Great Grandmother was there holding his hand and humming. The doctor had told Mama ahead of time that the surgery would be very tricky. Mama learned later when it was over, he'd flat lined twice but they were able to bring him back.

When the surgeon explained everything that happened, he told Mama he'd never felt anything like it before. He said from the time he walked into the operating room, he knew he felt a presence; he just had no idea where it was coming from. He said the room was almost electrical, to the point it made him sweat more. He even had the room checked before starting surgery to make sure there were no power problems. Mama said he teared up as he explained how he felt hands on top of his hands during the surgery. It was like he was being guided throughout the entire procedure. He said before he ever began, he felt peace that everything would be alright.

Looking back on the supernatural events that transpired with Daddy during those early years, I'm really not surprised. Daddy was one of the most faithful men I've ever known; faithful to pray, faithful to read his Bible, faithful in attending church, and faithful to his God. I've seen that man hurting so bad he could hardly move but he still went to church. He really believed in the teachings he'd grown up with and known. Honestly, with what I've been blessed to learn, I don't think it's so much what your religion is or being religious; it's just having faith in the higher power you believe in.

Even after all he'd been through and was going through, Daddy still held a full time job. He worked and kept up with the yard, garden, and animals, as well as his positions he held in our church. I remember many days seeing him come home with blood puddled up in his shoes from hemorrhaging. He would take a shower and put his clothes in the washing machine. Mama made up a special solution to soak them in before washing, to help get the blood out.

Many times Daddy came home pale as a ghost, other times he'd look sort of jaundice; I even remember the ashen look as well. It was hard for Mama not to always worry that something would happen to him. Bless her heart those early years set the pace for her to become a chronic worrier. Looking back now, the older she got, the more she worried; not just about daddy but about everything. It wasn't easy being on constant alert but for many years it was the only way we knew how to be.

Daddy didn't always have bad days though. There were some good times as well; those just seemed few and far between. He might have several days of feeling pretty good, then it would hit him, and he would have another kidney stone. The sickness and pain associated with it could last for days or weeks, most of the time showing no mercy. I remember several really bad times when Daddy had more than one stone. Unless you've experienced it for yourself, you cannot possibly imagine how the body is affected. Many nights he walked the yard for hours because he couldn't sleep. He said his back hurt so bad he could get no rest at all.

During an especially bad time, I had one of my first encounters with the power of prayer and the Spirit world. Daddy had been sick for a couple of weeks. He'd hemorrhaged something terrible from his kidney; he'd been in and out of the hospital. The doctor finally told Mama to take him home because they'd done all they could do for him; the blood flow just would not completely stop. That same evening the Preacher from the Church of God down the road came by. He brought the Elders of his church with him to pray for Daddy. He was a nice man and many times he'd stopped for a little talk when we were working in the yard or the garden. I remember Daddy giving him tomatoes on many occasions because he loved tomato sandwiches.

Daddy was weak but insisted on coming into the front living room. No one ever went in there except for piano playing, walking through to get the mail, and an occasional ladies circle meeting.

I honestly don't think that room was ever used but a handful of times until after Mama was gone; boy do we use it now. Mama kept the room in pristine shape in case of company. When company came though, they always sat in the den, so it remained one of those rooms just for show as we would say.

Daddy and I sat on my piano stool. Why he chose to sit there, I have no idea. Lord knows there was plenty of couch space. Maybe he knew Mama really didn't like anyone sitting on the sectional. My best guess would be he was bleeding so much he didn't want to take a chance on staining it, even though Mama kept the plastic on it for twenty five years. I watched as the men formed a circle to begin prayer. They asked God to be with them as they interceded for Mr. Chris and his needs. After the opening prayer, each man came forth and performed the laying on of hands. The Laying on of Hands is defined as a symbolic act that sets individuals apart and signifies the imparting of spiritual blessings, authority, and or power. I'd seen this done many times already in my short years with my Daddy participating as well, but never had I experienced the power this ritual contained until that day.

None of the men spoke out loud when their turn came and the energy in the room was nothing short of amazing. It was like nothing I'd ever felt before. Even as young as I was, I knew something supernatural was about to happen. Many prayers were sent up on Daddy's behalf by those men who gathered. I have no doubt what so ever, they really believed they could bring intercession on that day.

Mama had a lamp on each of the two end tables. About half way through praying, those lamps began to flicker. One detail I remember is what happened with Mama's organ. Mama had a small chord organ in the corner of the room. Whenever she would turn the organ on, it made a certain whistling sound for a few seconds; after it warmed up it would stop. I distinctly remember hearing that sound when the lights began to flicker. When I looked over, the light on the organ was on although no one was anywhere near it. Mama always kept it unplugged when not using it.

It was an amazing experience just to be a part of that day and something you never forget. I've had people who are not familiar with these practices ask me if it's real. I've said on many occasions that it's as real as the day is long, although this type of experience was not a common everyday occurrence. Whenever I think about that day's happenings, it always leads me back to this verse in the Bible, "For where two or three are gathered together in My name, there am I in the midst of them. Matthew 18:20." I'll talk more on this verse later.

Like a lot of children my age, I couldn't keep my eyes closed. I knew they should've been but I wanted to see what was taking place. When all the Elders finished praying, it was the Preacher's turn; he stood in front of Daddy and looked him straight in the eyes. "Mr. Chris, you're a good man and I believe with all my heart that God rewards good deeds to those who are faithful to believe in Him. As God's prayer warriors, we are claiming that power here and now in this very room. We believe that you will find your strength again and the flow of blood will stop." Then he closed his eyes, placed his hands on the top of Daddy's head, and silently prayed. It's not hard to recall those times when you've heard the stories retold over and over.

Now this is where the supernatural really gets interesting, and those of you who have witnessed a similar occurrence will understand. I began to feel heat, like I was warming up. Then my body began to tingle, almost like an electric current shooting through. As Daddy held my hand, I could feel his body tingling next to mine. I don't mind telling you, I was scared to death; I had no idea what was about to happen. I felt a wave of fire go all over my body. It came out of Daddy's right arm and into my left arm. I felt a rocking movement like we were going to fall but we didn't. Then I watched as my piano stool rose up off the floor about 2 inches, hovered for a moment, and gently sat back down.

You can only imagine what was going through my mind. Even as a small child, I knew it was the power of God, the Universe, the Creator, or whatever you choose to call it by; it was powerful. The energy contained in the room that day was unforgettable. Daddy's color almost immediately looked better and after they left, he ate well for the first time in a week. The most fascinating part of the whole experience was the bleeding from the kidney area immediately ceased. Daddy said he felt it stop as the piano stool rose up off the floor.

I have no doubt in my mind that power reached out to everyone in the room that day. My mother had suffered terribly with a headache for almost a week because of worry, stress, and exhaustion from sitting at the hospital. She told us later that evening, she also saw the piano stool rise up off the floor. Mama said she felt power radiate out into the room and her headache was gone. I would learn later, after my own near death experience, about the power of prayer and the real power of those that stand together and pray in numbers.

Not long after that sacred experience, we were working in the yard one day. One of the church elders who prayed stopped by. Daddy took off his gloves and shook the man's hand. He told us he prayed before coming to our house that morning for his own body to be healed of cancer. He'd known it was bad for quite some time; he'd hoped God would have mercy on him as well. His reason for stopping by was to say his cancer was completely gone. It was a truly miraculous day and since then, we've had numerous supernatural occurrences in this house.

Many times, especially if it's raining, I experience what some would call strange happenings. I've had friends who've been here to witness these occurrences. My children will tell you of things that have happened here, like a particular light flickering on and off, yet the bulb is fine. Even when the bulb is changed, it happens again; usually when we're talking about Mama or Daddy or someone who has gone on home. From the research I've done, when a house has had a supernatural occurrence and the amount of energy like what happened on that day flows through, it remains there forever. Sometimes it still sends a wave of energy through my body. As of this moment, the light on my desk has been flickering on and off for about five minutes.

The intense energy that each of us experienced that day, along with my own near death experience, left me with what I would call hindrances as well. Although good came from both of them, I find myself being rough on equipment; especially cell phones and chargers. One of my best friends and co-worker Leah, can attest to the fact that I go through these things like there's no tomorrow. Electrical gadgets tend to act up sometimes when I'm around. I've had phones go haywire, and TVs and radios turn on and off; my printer turns on at random times as well. Just a couple of weeks ago, I was in the kitchen washing dishes and the microwave just turned itself on. It went through a two minute cycle. The energy associated with prayer and miracles is powerful and it remains.

I tell you these things because I want you to know, if you don't already, just how very powerful prayer is and the energy associated with it. All of us who believe in prayer believe that our prayers are heard. If we didn't believe, what would be the point, right? Maybe the outcome is not necessarily as we pray for it, but we believe that God hears our prayers. I can tell you that all prayers are heard and the importance of praying should be at the top of our list.

There are studies being conducted right now about the power of "Group Thinking." It's basically a group of people banding together at predetermined times, thinking about the same outcome for a situation. Sometimes, the people participating are scattered all over the place. For the ones of you who follow Coast to Coast radio, they've done this on several occasions. One particular time, there were hundreds of Coast listeners who prayed for rain because of the drought in California; when it finally did rain, it flooded. Praying in numbers is basically the same thing. It's the same exact experience that happened in our living room that day; there are verses in the Bible that support that. Believe me folks, it's not just a theory; it's fact. I've seen and experienced it firsthand many times.

Whatever version of the Bible you choose to read, Matthew 18:20 tells us this same thing, "For where two or three are gathered in my name, there am I among them." Does this mean if we pray alone our prayers are meaningless or have less power? Certainly not; as I said before, every prayer is heard. As with anything else, if you want something, you've got to work for it. For example, if someone you know has a health problem and asks for prayers, then grab your family and friends together. Pray your heart out for that person. Be grateful he or she thought enough of you to ask for prayers. For those of you on Facebook, you know how someone is always asking for prayers for themselves and for others. Many times, I'm sure you've later read where there was a good outcome. I'd like to think all the many folks banding together to pray had something to do with it too. Another good verse is Matthew 18:19, "Again I say to you, if two of you agree on earth about anything they ask, it will be done for them by my Father in Heaven." Wow! Could there be a more powerful statement than that?

Many of you, like me, can probably think of one or two people in particular. You know beyond the shadow of a doubt, they are faithful praying souls. When you ask them to pray and they tell you they will, there is no doubt whatsoever in your mind your need will be prayed about. Not only that, they get on the phone and you can call it gossiping or whatever but they will start their usual prayer chain of praying people. I have several dear souls that I can always count on in my life. When I need prayer, believe me I'm the first to start calling on my prayer warriors.

A couple of years ago, I had the privilege of talking with a young man who'd been diagnosed with an inoperable brain tumor. My heart ached for him and what he was going through. He worked at one of the truck stops we always fueled at. Even though he was dealing with this horrible issue, at the time he was still able to work. He told me one day about how some of the students at his school were holding special prayer services for him. For four months, anyone who would take the time to pray would meet on Monday, Wednesday, and Thursday mornings. Each member would touch his head and pray. Last I talked with him, he told me his brain tumor had shrunk up to the size of a small prune; he was doing fantastic. Prayer is free folks, it does a body good.

Chapter Three

Shot and Left for Dead

It was a typical Saturday morning at our house. Mama loved her Saturdays; she could clean, wash, and hang out clothes all day if she wanted too. Daddy got up with the chickens as usual and had just finished mowing the yard. The weather was perfect, we were going fishing. Normally we would've worked in the yard all day, but Daddy was itching to catch some fish and have a big ole fish fry at Nannie and Papas. Any other time, my Papa would've gone too but he'd been a little under the weather. Daddy said it'd be just us two and we'd catch Papa a mess of fish to make him feel better. It was always exciting going to Nannie and Papa's for a fish fry.

Daddy threw the cane poles in back of his old blue Chevy truck. It seemed like the sun had just made a good appearance that morning when he showed me the old rusty coffee can. He'd dug up some of the fattest worms earlier in the garden while it was still dark. Daddy had a theory; if you dug the worms before the sun fully rose, the fish would bite better. It must have been a pretty good notion because we always caught a mess every time we went; he said his Grandpa taught him that.

I was so excited I almost fell trying to climb in with the tackle box and net. Mama came out carrying a bag of egg salad sandwiches that she'd made and a jug of ice cold water. This time though, she handed me brownies made with pecans from our tree. Daddy had another theory too; pecans made anything good, that much better.

I could hardly wait because fishing was probably my most favorite thing in the world to do; we went a lot. Daddy never had sons, so from an early age he taught me his secrets of the greatest pastime ever. Even though I was a girl, I'd gotten pretty good at catching those brim and catfish. I never liked baiting that hook, still don't. I can see him chuckling now as I dug one of those old fat night crawlers out of the can; I cringed every time. Daddy had one rule, never fish for sport. We never wasted one single catch; we ate them all.

While munching on one of those delicious brownies I'd dug out of the bag, I noticed my best friend Jennifer running across the road. She stayed with our neighbors some. We played together all the time. I wanted so bad to go fishing with Daddy but playing outside with my best friend was calling my name as well. It wasn't often we had a good Saturday of getting into mischief.

Daddy came out of the house carrying a couple of bags. Fishing was serious business, so we had to be prepared. He said his good morning to Jennifer and suggested we play for a while. He'd go on down to the river and see if the fish were biting; he felt that would be better. "No need in traipsing through the briars if you don't have too," he said, "they may not be hungry." He promised if the biting was good, he'd head back and pick me up. Little did we know, Jennifer probably saved my life on that fateful day.

It sounded like a pretty good plan to us, so we waved goodbye running off toward the playhouse. Mama never allowed playing inside because she didn't like things messed up, so we knew better than to ask. That was Daddy's main reason a couple of years before for building me a huge playhouse. It was a 20 x 20 building and I'd rather have been in that playhouse, than my own room anytime.

Looking back on it now, a person could have lived in that thing. Daddy invented the tiny house and didn't even know it.

After playing for a while, we ran in the house to get a drink. It was then I noticed the time on the clock; it had been two hours since Daddy left. Mama was still busy doing her annual spring cleaning. I couldn't imagine what was taking him so long. I asked Mama reckon why Daddy had not come back to get me yet? She said he was probably at my Uncle Richards talking. "You know how your Daddy is," she said, "I'll call and find him." So Jennifer and I went back outside to play.

All of a sudden we spotted Daddy's truck coming, but something was strange about it. It was like he was weaving back and forth from one side to the other. Jennifer and I watched as he made his way up the road beside our house to the stop sign. We ran around to catch him as he pulled into the driveway. I figured Mama had told my Aunt to send him on home. We frowned as he ran all over the shrubbery; I knew I'd never seen him drive like that before.

We ran to meet him, but what we saw looked like something out of a horror movie. There in the seat, was a figure completely covered with blood; you could barely see the whites of his eyes. We stood there frozen, not knowing what to say or do. When he opened the door he just fell out on the ground. I screamed, "Daddy what's wrong?" About that time I saw one of our neighbors pulling into the driveway. He'd seen Daddy come up the road driving crazy and decided to check on him.

I ran in to where Mama was cleaning. She was sitting on the kitchen floor wiping chair legs; I stopped dead in my tracks. "Donna Kaye, I know you didn't just let that door slam young lady," she said. I told her that Daddy was back but something was wrong with him, she jumped up and ran out of the house.

By the time Mama got to Daddy, more neighbors had shown up. Someone called the Rescue Squad but in all the confusion, I have no idea who it was. Mama almost fainted when she saw how bad he looked. She kneeled down beside him, frantically trying to find out what had happened. By this time, two of my Uncles were pulling in the driveway. Our neighbor had called them and said something bad happened. Mama was crying and screaming. She tried desperately to wipe the blood from his eyes but he just laid there; he never moved. Honestly, I thought he was dead. I'm sure Mama did too.

The Rescue Squad raced into our driveway. They opened the door on the ambulance and began grabbing equipment out the back. It seemed like only seconds went by before they had him hooked up to all kinds of machines. One of the men asked if anyone knew what could possibly have happened. No one knew for sure but Mama said he must have been hemorrhaging from his kidney; at least that's what we all thought.

Daddy had lost so much blood; his clothes were soaking wet with the dark red stains. My Uncle said he must have fallen in the river. Mama kept asking the men if he was still alive. One of them told her he was but she didn't believe him; she was hysterical. He took her hand and put it on daddy's neck. "Betty, he's still alive because he's got a faint pulse but we have to get him to the hospital now," he said.

We watched in disbelief and confusion as they loaded him into the ambulance. Mama and I followed with some of the family right behind them. Mama talked with my Aunt and Uncle on the way about how much blood Daddy had lost. She said they would probably have to do some type of surgery on his kidney to stop the hemorrhaging, if they could even get it to stop. No one ever considered any other possibility for the blood loss. We had no idea of what really happened at that point.

We sat eagerly awaiting any news of Daddy's condition. After a while, that waiting took its toll on Mama's nerves; she couldn't sit still. She paced back and forth, waiting for news whether good or not so good. I always hated the waiting part, it was awful. Mama's saying was, "You never know what you're going to hear when they walk through that door." By this time several family members had shown up, including my Daddy's brothers and our Preacher.

About the time Mama was ready to fall apart, the doctor finally came out. He explained that the blood did not come from his kidney. "He's been shot in the head; we're sure it was an arrow." At that point you could have heard a pin drop with that news. Everyone stared at each other with looks of disbelief over what they had heard. "Are you sure?" my Uncle asked. "I have no explanation for this, other than we're sure it was an arrow; it's been sent to the lab for testing. We could only get so much of it out; now we're trying to control the bleeding," The doctor said Daddy would need to be transported to another hospital, where they were better equipped to handle trauma situations of that degree.

By the time he was finished talking, they were loading him up for the trip. We ran to the parking lot, jumped in my Uncle's car, and took off for Greenville. It was about fifteen miles away but that fifteen miles seemed like two hundred; I thought we'd never get there.

The emergency parking area was packed. Mama checked in only to be told Daddy was already being prepped for surgery. The nurse handed her a stack of papers to sign; I was sure that was the last thing on her mind. Everybody sat down and basically stared at each other. No one knew what to say; it was all a blur. I can remember my uncles talking among themselves. I think they had to talk it out so as not to go crazy. One of them left to go down to the river. He said he had to try and make some sense of what had happened.

Daddy stayed in surgery for over five hours. During that time our town's Police Chief came by. He said he'd got the call about Daddy being shot; he came by to find out how he was doing. Mama told him Daddy was in surgery and his condition was serious. When the doctor finally finished, he told us they'd gone in and removed the rest of the arrow pieces from his head. The bleeding had stopped but his condition was grave. We were told he'd lost approximately 4-5 pints of blood. "Judging from the amount of blood loss he should have already been dead," the Doctor said, "we've stopped the bleeding for now; he's receiving blood. If you are praying people, I suggest you pray hard."

Word of what happened to Daddy spread like wildfire. No one could believe something this horrible could happen to anyone in our town. Dozens of people filed into the emergency waiting area that day: family, church family, friends that Mama and Daddy worked with all came by to lend support and prayers. My Uncle came back from the river; he said police cars were everywhere, searching the places Daddy fished the most.

The Doctor said Daddy would remain in ICU for the next few days, if he made it. He told us the first forty eight hours were critical. People were praying with us and for us. Poor Mama, she almost broke down several times. I know it wasn't an easy situation for her; she'd been through so much with him already. He'd not long been over the last bad bout with his kidney.

Later that day Daddy was moved to ICU. Back then it was a lot different than now; I couldn't even see him, children weren't allowed. It was only immediate family members and only for a couple of minutes at a time. I remember feeling so sad because I couldn't go with Mama. I kept thinking I would probably never get to see him again; he would die without me saying, "I love you."

I rode home with my Aunt and Uncle. I asked if they would take me to my Grandparent's house; it was just where I needed to be. Shortly after we got there, another Uncle stopped by on his way home from the hospital. He couldn't believe how bad Daddy looked. He told my Grandparents that his color was gray. He said whoever shot Daddy had kicked him so hard in the chest it left bruises the shape of boot prints.

Papa was so angry and Nannie was crying. She asked Buddy to take her to the hospital to be with Mama. Papa was to keep an eye on me. She'd be back as soon as she could. She made sure there was plenty of food in the ice box, but neither of us had any kind of appetite; I felt so sick at my stomach. I just couldn't believe anyone would do something so horrible. I asked Papa why somebody would want to hurt him. Papa just stared ahead as he whittled, "I don't know child."

That evening my Aunt took me home with her. She thought it would do me good to play with my cousins. I didn't feel like playing or doing anything, I was just numb. I was so worried about daddy, my whole body seemed cold; I was shaking. I'm fifty two years old now and my body still reacts the same way when I'm really worried about something. My Aunt wrapped me up in a blanket when we got home. She told me not to worry that everything would be okay. She said she had faith that Daddy would be fine because lots of people were praying for him; she told me to pray too.

I hardly slept at all that night, it was awful. The next morning I heard Mama talking in the kitchen, they were drinking coffee. Mama was telling my Aunt what she knew. I walked in and sat down beside her; she smiled and asked if I was okay. I gave her a little smile back and nodded that I was. I wasn't okay; I just didn't want her to worry about me. Mama had left the hospital long enough to come home, take a bath, change clothes, and check on me; she was headed back after that.

Two days had passed when the doctors gave Mama some hope. Daddy seemed to be a strong man, a fighter, so all they could do was wait and see. Daddy grew a tiny bit stronger with each passing day; a week later, they were hopeful he would pull through. We were told to keep the prayers coming because they seemed to be working. I remember Mama talking with one Doctor. She got special permission for the Church of God Elders to come and pray for him. They all came; they hung a sign on the door that read, "Healing in Progress."

Mama said that people from all over were praying for Daddy. Several churches in our area were having special prayers that he would regain his strength and pull through. I remember our church family being so kind to us. Some of the men came by to cut grass and work the garden. Ladies from Mama's office came by with casseroles. We had so much food that Mama began freezing some of it. She said we'd save some for when Daddy came home.

I missed Daddy; it had been almost two weeks since he'd been home. I overheard talking about the bruises on his body. My Aunt said she'd never seen anything so horrible; my Uncles were so upset. Although my Daddy was a peacemaker, he had brothers that didn't think the same way he did about something so horrible. They were fine men, I loved them all but their main goal was finding out who had done this horrible deed. They wouldn't rest until they did.

After almost three weeks, my Aunt picked me up one day from school. We headed to the hospital. Daddy was awake and asking for me, I was so excited. Mama got special permission for me to visit. As I said before, when I was young hospital rules were much different than they are now. I didn't care if I could only stay five minutes; I just wanted to see him.

Mama warned me in advance how bad he looked. She said his color wasn't right and he had lots of bruises. She told me not to let on if I could help it because it would just upset him. As we got closer to his room, my stomach knotted up; I knew it would be hard to see him. I took a deep breath while gripping my Aunt's hand even tighter. Daddy was sleeping but everything Mama said was right. He looked awful; his color had a grayish hue. There were scabs on his face and around his lips where he'd been kicked and hit. Both eyes were black, and when I say black, I mean black. He looked thinner than normal; his face, chest, and hands were badly bruised as well.

It was all I could do not to cry. Even at such a young age, I was so angry that someone could commit a crime so evil. I kept asking myself why someone would want to hurt Daddy. He was so kind to everyone, helping whoever was in need. I can remember my Mama and Aunt discussing all the bad in the world. Mama talked of how we lived in a small town and we knew everybody; it just didn't make sense to her.

A week later Daddy came home and what a homecoming it was. Everybody dropped by to say hello: friends from church, work, neighbors, teachers, and family came. Mama definitely didn't have to worry about cooking for a while. Daddy sat in his recliner; he loved it and stayed there for several days. He said it was easier to get in and out of because of being so sore. I asked if I could see the boot print on his chest. Mama said no, but Daddy told her it was okay. It was a huge print, perfectly outlined which meant he'd been stomped on really hard. I'd never seen anything like that before.

It didn't take long for our local Police Chief, his officers, and some new people to come by. They talked with daddy and asked him to recall any details he could think of so that it would help their investigation. They were all kind to us. They knew he still had a ways to go in getting his strength back. They also wanted to talk with him while it was fresh in his mind.

There was a lady I'd never seen before writing things down as Daddy talked; a strange man in a suit was asking questions. They told him not to wear himself out, just do what he could. The following is a partial excerpt of what happened after he left the house the day he was attacked, in Daddy's own words. He kept his copy for many years in his dresser drawer. Many times I snuck it out so I could read it; I have no idea why, I just did.

Daddy: I left my house around eleven am on Saturday. I drove up town to pick up a couple of things, got gas in my truck, went by the church, and drove to Big Creek Road down to the river. I parked my truck off the side of the road and carried my tackle box and one of my fishing poles with me. I wanted to see if the fish were biting before bringing my Daughter because of the briars. I baited my hook, threw it in, and settled down to wait. Across the river I could see two men sitting there. They weren't fishing, just sitting. I waved and they waved back.

Police: Mr. Davenport did you recognize either of the two men sitting there?

Daddy: Yes

Police: Were they friends of yours or did you just know of them?

Daddy: I consider everybody I know a friend but I only knew one of the men.

Daddy: I sat there about fifteen minutes and I'd already caught two fish. I decided I would leave my pole and tackle box and go home to get my daughter. When I was getting up I looked across to the other side again and the men were gone. I didn't think much about it. When I stood up, I felt a sharp pain in the back of my head and I fell to the ground. I remember feeling something wet on my face; when I rubbed my hand on back of my head there was blood everywhere. I tried to stand up but I was knocked down by somebody. I could hear a man talking, He said, "He won't last long with that blow to the head, he'll bleed to death."

I tried again to stand up but this time I felt a hard kick to my kidney area. My vision was blurry and I could hardly see. Then I felt somebody going through my pockets. I could hear them talking. One said, "Yeah we hit the jackpot, he just got paid yesterday." Then I heard my keys rattling then hitting the water. I knew they had thrown them in the river. Then a man started stomping my chest. He kicked me several times in the chest, back, and kidney area, I felt blows to my face.

Police: Mr. Davenport how long would you say this assault lasted?

Daddy: Several minutes

Daddy: After that I thought they were gone. I didn't hear them talking anymore and I could barely move. I heard somebody walking, coming closer to me; I knew it was them. One of the men said, "He's almost gone, let's just push him in the river and let him drown." I felt them dragging me and then they rolled me into the water.

Police: Mr. Davenport about how far would you say you were dragged? Approximately how many feet were you from the water by this time?

Daddy: About six feet.

Daddy: I knew when I hit the water I was in trouble. I've always been a good swimmer but my head was hurting so bad I was going in and out; I knew I was going to pass out. I remember floating down the river; the water was so cold. I must have passed out for a few minutes, I don't really know if I did or not. Then I felt myself hit something. My whole body was caught on something big. I could feel it was a tree or log that had fell. I didn't know how I was going to get myself free, much less climb out. I hurt so bad all I wanted to do was go to sleep. I started praying the Lord's Prayer as best I could. I just kept falling asleep but I kept on saying that prayer. Then I felt a hand on my shoulder. It was my Grandpa and he said, "Chris, you've got to get up now, it's time to get up." I talked to him for a minute and told him I was hurt bad and I couldn't get up. He patted me on the shoulder again and said, "Yes you can son, you're strong and you can get up. You've got a lot to live for."

Police: So your Grandpa found you?

Daddy: My Grandpa died a long time ago.

At this point when Daddy said that his Grandpa died a long time ago, there was total silence for a moment. Everybody just looked at each other.

Daddy: I must have gone to sleep again for a few minutes. Then I heard Grandpa talking again telling me to get up son. I tried but my leg was stuck under the log. Then I felt a pull and my leg came loose. I prayed and asked God to give me strength enough just to get up and somehow get home. I managed to climb out of the water onto the river bank. I must have passed out again for a while because I remember going to sleep. While I was sleeping I saw family telling me that everything would be okay just to rest a minute. Grandpa was there, he stayed right beside me. I dreamed of the many times I went fishing when I was just a boy. I woke up; my head was splitting open and when I tried to stand up I was so dizzy I could barely see because there was so much blood. I took my handkerchief out of my pocket and wiped my eyes. I could barely see up the river bank, my truck was there and I knew I had a spare key taped under the dash in case I needed it. It took me a long time to get back up to my truck, but I did. I got in and I don't remember putting the key in or starting it up. I don't remember driving home either. I just remember pulling in my driveway. That's all I remember about it.

When Daddy gave his statement, Papa and all my Uncles were there; you could've heard a pin drop. You could see the fire in their eyes; they were out for blood. I remember the Police Chief telling them not to do something stupid; they would catch whoever did this. Daddy didn't get to finish talking to them because he was just so weak. He could barely stay awake by this time. The men told Daddy to rest; they would come back the next day and finish. Mama thanked them for coming and they assured her everything would be okay.

One of my Uncles knelt down beside Daddy's chair. "Chris, who was the man you knew?" Daddy just closed his eyes and went to sleep. After that, Mama scooted them all out. Everyone gathered in the driveway for a bit. I could hear them talking about finding whoever had done this to him.

Daddy slept most of the next day. The Police Chief came by but Mama asked if it could possibly wait another day because he was just so weak. He assured her that was fine; he'd call before coming by. That afternoon Mama kept busy washing and hanging out clothes. I watched TV in the den with Daddy. I think we all were so eager just to get back into some kind of normal routine.

The phone rang and Mama answered it before I could. She got the strangest look on her face while talking. "My husband had an accident and he's not well." She stepped around the corner and told Daddy that some man insisted on talking to him. He said it was fine so she handed him the phone.

Mama and I watched Daddy; we listened to maybe hear who it was. He didn't say a word, then handed Mama the receiver back. "Who in the world was that?" she asked. Daddy had the most horrible look on his face. We didn't know what was going on but something had clearly stirred him up. He told me to go to my room that he needed to talk to Mama for a minute. I did as I was told but had no idea why he didn't want me in there.

I heard Mama make a call; it didn't take long for the Police Chief to get there. He came inside; I could hear them talking because I was listening. Daddy told him he'd received a call from one of the men that shot him. He said he could tell the man was reading from his driver's license. He read his full name and address to him over the phone; he told daddy to listen and listen good. He said he knew Daddy could identify him and if he did, the same thing would happen to his Daughter. He assured Daddy I wouldn't live to tell about it.

By this time my Mama was frantic; she was crying and inconsolable. She yelled for me and gave me strict instructions not to go outside without her and she meant it. Mama called her brother; it didn't take long for him and my other uncles to get there. It was a nightmare for our family for quite a while. Daddy refused to give the police or anyone else a name. He said he wouldn't do it because he had to protect me. My uncles urged him to say who it was but he wouldn't.

I don't know if our family ever did know normal again after that. It affected us to the point that Mama became cautious of even leaving the house. After a few months, things died down and Daddy got better. He eventually started fishing again but not on the river bank. He only went to open areas where people were at. He said Mama laid the law down to him. He knew Mama would never hear of it being any other way.

When I was much older, Daddy and I were reminiscing one day about happenings through the years. In conversation I mentioned those dark days. I asked Daddy straight up to tell me who the man was that shot him; at first he was hesitant to do it.

I explained that I needed to know for my own peace of mind, so he told me. I often thought of that secret he carried with him all those years. Only a couple of people ever knew. Thinking back, that must have been hard for him to live with. He would have done anything for his family. That's one of the many qualities that defined him.

I asked Daddy if it was hard living with what happened to him that day. "Does it ever bother you that he never paid for what he did?" I asked. He was putting a new line on a fishing pole and never missed a beat. He just looked up at me and said, "Aww honey, I'm not worried about it, the Good Lord will deal with him in his own time." From what I heard later on in years, He did.

Chapter Four

My Journey-Part One

After Daddy's accident, my family went through many years of ups and downs with his health. Bless his heart, he did the best he could but there were days I know he just wanted to go on home. I have no doubt whatsoever Daddy's main reason for fighting the way he did was because of his family; we always had a connection. The kindred love we had only got stronger with the years that passed. I grew up and life happened to me; I went through many ups and downs myself. I was lucky that Daddy was always there to offer his sage advice, or just plain out tell me what I should do. Many times he exercised his right as my Dad to do that.

The time did eventually come when he was granted a reprieve from his ongoing health problems. He saw it as grace, and considering the hell he'd been through most of his life, who were we to say any different? I was so grateful for those good years; at least he got to really enjoy life during that time.

After my Near Death Experience, the openness I had with Daddy began to fade somewhat. It was a time in my life where he could no longer offer advice, matter of fact I couldn't talk to him much at all about it. In many ways he was oblivious to what I was going through, even though he'd experienced something similar on a couple of different occasions. One thing was for certain though, our love remained the same. The next few years would become a time of growth for me; years where I would step out of the shoes of religion and into the shoes of finding my spiritual side. Some things Daddy understood, but others he'd just stare like he was confused. He stood firm in his old beliefs, the beliefs he was raised with; he wasn't about to budge. Little did I know, I was about to start a new journey. One in which I would become so much closer with Mama, closer than we'd ever been before in my life.

Those of you familiar with near death experiences know by now there are hundreds, if not thousands of recorded accounts. Only after my experience did I realize I'd actually been a witness to this remarkable undertaking growing up. I spent many hours in the beginning pondering over that episode in my life, trying to make sure I remembered every detail. In doing so, I found I didn't have to try and remember. It just came to me naturally; it was engrained in my mind. After having my own experience, I finally understood what happened to Daddy. We never put the NDE label on what happened to him. Back then we didn't call it that; it was just labeled as a miraculous happening.

Writing this chapter was very difficult for me. Honestly, it was the most time consuming one of all. In the short span of crossing over and coming back, I witnessed so much. Some parts were not so good, let's face it they were horrible. Still other parts were nothing short of wonderful and miraculous. I wish I could share with you every detail, but I can't. Some I won't share until I feel like my corner of the world is ready. Still there are other parts I don't remember, but I know they existed. When I get flashes and tidbits of those parts, and it happens a lot, it's fuzzy. I'm sure it's because those elements of my experience have been erased. We're just not meant to know everything while we're here. With that being said, this chapter brought about many emotions. It's impossible to experience something of this magnitude and brush it off like it's nothing. Your human side wants to share that experience with those you care about. That's what we do, we share important events.

In reading the rest of my story, I can only hope you will be kind. Please understand, it's written based on what happened to me and what I witnessed. It's different from other accounts in so many ways, but also so similar to many others. Please refrain from passing judgement simply because you don't agree or understand. Just keep an open mind to the possibility that sometimes things are different. I wouldn't take a million dollars for my religious upbringing. It set the pace for my outlook and treatment of others in this life; but in the end it's up to us. If we want to advance closer to God, to find out what life's mysteries hold, then we have to step outside our safe zone. It's like being in school and advancing your studies. I'm not asking for you to believe or disbelieve anything you read. Just remember that I was like many of you in terms of my belief system until it happened to me.

After my NDE and getting over the initial shock, I began doing my own research. I've read hundreds of near death accounts. As I said, some are remarkably similar, some a little different, and some very different. I've found in researching that no two are exactly alike but all have a common theme. That theme is love, peace, hope, and all the good stuff that goes along with it. Even those who experienced torment knew that love was the only way. I'll ask you to remember one important aspect. Where we go when it's our time, is based on our belief system. I witnessed many different spiritual themes, some I wasn't even familiar with. I saw Hindus meditating in Temples, Christians attending worship services in Churches much like what we see here, Buddhist monks who had achieved "Nirvana," Muslims attending Mosque, as well as Nature People worshiping in the outdoors.

I was so confused at first; I had no idea why I'd seen all those different religions, as I labeled them. I would probably still be searching for the answer if not for my Guardian Angel Rachel. I'll never forget what she said to me, "You must remember that your beliefs are not the only path to God. There are many paths that exist, *some* based on your belief system. The number is so great it would do you well to study them. For ex: Buddhist do not experience the same as a Southern Baptist, or Pentecostal who is a Christian. Catholics do not experience the same thing as someone who practices Islam. It doesn't mean one is more right or wrong; it means there are many different beliefs. There are endless ways of returning to the Creator (God); the Source is known by many different names. There is good and not so good in everything, including religion. Your world was never supposed to be about religion in the first place. It was supposed to be about love and finding your spiritual path. Sadly, a great portion of your religion today is business. It lines the pockets of those who seek nothing but worldly possessions through greed."

Rachel showed me books of many different religions from around the world. Before me was the Tibetan Book of the Dead, the Torah, the Vedas, the Bible, the Quran, the Egyptian Book of the Dead, the Bhagavad Gita, and countless others. I was amazed, for I had never seen such a display. I didn't have a clue about any of them but the Bible. It was odd because I felt nothing but love coming from each and every one. Once again I heard her wise words, "At times when one is taught there is only one road, one misses out on the many wonders the Universe holds. If you are traveling a main road each trip to get to a certain destination, you will only see what is on the main road. If you sometimes take a slight detour onto another road, then you will also find beauty and treasures on that road as well. The teachings of the Creator are meant for all, for in the beginning, God (as you call the Creator), made everything and it was a diverse creation. We are all different, yet the same in so many ways."

Before writing this chapter, I prayed and asked for guidance. I only wanted to include what is most beneficial to you as the reader. I've learned to ask for guidance in everything and it always comes in some form. We must search our hearts and trust that

God, the Creator, or whatever term you choose to use is always there for us, guiding and teaching as we walk this path called life.

I remember feeling extremely tired, like I could sleep for days. I'd been sick with what I thought was an upper respiratory infection because my chest seemed congested. It was a cold January day, we were getting ready to leave out on a trucking run. My husband went out to start the car and load our bags; he said he'd make a couple of calls while waiting on me. I told him I'd wrap things up in the house and be out shortly. I'd said my goodbyes to all the kids earlier, assuring them we'd be back in a few days; they were grown by this time. While walking through the dining room, I felt a fire like sensation go through my chest along with a sharp pain; then there was nothing. No pain, no sound, no light, just nothing for what seemed like a few seconds.

I never remember going through a tunnel or seeing a light, although I know I did. I wasn't fully aware of what was happening at first, but I wasn't afraid because all I felt was peace and love. Just a lightweight feeling, almost like I was being rocked to sleep in big, comfortable arms. I was aware of passing through some type of levels. Later on I would learn in depth what these levels are that make up the Other Side. I felt warmth on my face, so comforting I don't even have words to describe it. I couldn't see the sun shining but there was light everywhere. I felt grass beneath my feet, so soft and plush it felt like carpet. There were trees, beautiful rolling green hills, a river, and the most gorgeous colors of flowers I'd ever seen. Some of the colors I saw are not here and I have no words to describe their hue.

There were butterflies, birds, and children playing. It brought me great comfort to hear them laughing while running and chasing after each other. There were animals there; puppies were running and chasing balls as children threw them. I saw my Nannie as she waved and smiled. She looked the best I'd ever seen her, like she was younger and so beautiful. My Papa was also there along with several family members and friends I'd known; they were all busy across the river. The setting reminded me of a quaint little Southern town preparing for some type of big celebration.

There was a presence close to me; I knew who it was by the energy. I later learned that we are all made up of energy. We each carry a certain vibration; it's like a handprint, and all are different. The angel's energy is different from humans for example. I felt a hand on my shoulder and from her touch, I knew it was Rachel. Remember I first met her when I was five in the hospital ER waiting area. She really didn't have to talk to me. It's like I could almost read her thoughts, but some were a little unclear. She told me we would communicate in the manner I was accustomed to. When you first cross back over, it takes a while to readjust to your surroundings. As a rule, angels are non-gender. They present themselves in ways you identify with the most, depending on your particular situation. Those helpful beings from the Other Side just know what you need and when you need it.

Rachel graciously welcomed me back home. I knew when I felt the grass beneath my feet, all was as it should be. Where we are now, here on Earth, is not home. It's just temporary; then we go back. Rachel explained that most people are a little confused for a short time when they first return. She said you have to readjust and regain your boundaries. She assured me there are plenty of helpers and guides along the way. "So I died?" I asked. She stared at me with the kindest eyes. "No one dies; there is no such thing as death to the soul, only the body. Your heart simply grew tired. Sometimes when this happens it causes you to cross prematurely when it's not your time."

At this point I was really confused. Rachel showed me many scenes throughout my life where I'd had much stress; times I didn't take care of myself when I was sick. There were times I should have rested more but worked myself into a tizzy because of chores I felt had to be done. I've always been such a perfectionist. All these factors led up to my heart finally giving out. She showed me when my actual time would have been to exit from here and go back home. When I chose to come back, that memory was erased; I understand why now. I can't imagine being here and knowing the exact second my time would be up. I'm sure some people would love to know this but not me.

It was then I learned about the many different levels on the Other Side. What I experienced when I was crossing over, when everything was fuzzy, was the two lower levels. There were many levels, with Heaven being the top one. I couldn't see Heaven I just knew it was there. I couldn't see the lower levels from where I was at either but I knew they existed. I could hear faint moaning and all kinds of disturbing noises coming from the lower realms. I was curious, I asked if I could see them; Rachel said she didn't know if I would want to. I told her I felt I just needed to see for myself what was there. I didn't know why; I just needed to understand it. Rachel did some type of preparation. I honestly don't remember what it was. She called it a type of grounding that would protect me from the dark energies on those levels. She prepared me first by telling a little about those realms.

"The lowest realm is where you're going to find the most horrible of conditions. Think of it as your worst nightmare, something that scared you so bad you could hardly breathe; that's the lowest level. It's the level closest to Earth and the most distant from God. This level is where all demons live. They prey on those still living in the body while on Earth. But this only happens if they are allowed in." "Are you sure you want to go there?" she asked; I shook my head yes. Rachel explained that I would observe the most repulsive and cruelest of conditions, especially on the lower realm. She said she would be with me for the viewing but we would not be able to remain there for long because of the dark energies.

It was total darkness at first; it took a few minutes for my eyes to adjust. I saw disfigured images of different creatures roaming around. The atmosphere there was so heavy I could hardly breathe. I witnessed how these demons prey on their victims. People sometimes open themselves up to let bad things happen to them. I saw where people had used drugs and abused their bodies to the point of allowing these demons to take over. When this happens to someone, it's because they have allowed it through their dependence on a substance foreign to the body.

These demons play mind games; before you know it a person's mind has been taken over. These demons cause people to commit horrible acts against others. They stalk those in body form and magnify circumstances to make them worse; this level is void of any light. It's total darkness to the souls who reside there; it smells horrible. The feeling I got from just being there brought such a sick sense to my stomach. I felt nothing but pain and despair.

This is the realm where souls reside that are void of any love by their own choosing. They feel totally alone with no chance of love, hope, or peace. I felt sad for those who allowed this to happen because of the life they lived while on Earth. They created for themselves through their malevolent acts, nothing but hopelessness and despair while living. They were given many chances to make things right during their lifetimes of rage, anger, and hurt.

Ultimately when their time came to cross over, they were brought to this level so they could continue that hopelessness and despair. The only difference is they are now in a place where they experience all those malevolent feelings and despair within themselves. They can never harm another living soul. That's why it's important while living that we strive for love, peace, hope, and benevolence.

Rachel showed me two different scenes. In the first scene, I saw a man living a life of love. He lived by what we call the Fruits of the Spirit. His life was filled with kindness, peacefulness, and brotherly love; he practiced friendship and patience. When his time came to cross over, he went to a level similar to what he had lived while on the Earth. In the second scene I saw the same man living a life where he created nothing but fear; there was no love period. He lived by the rule of everything for himself, not caring who he hurt along the way. I saw him abusing others, both mentally and physically; compassion did not exist. His whole life was spent hurting those around him. When it came his time to cross over, he went to this lower level because it was similar to what he had created for himself while on earth.

I asked if people who commit horrible acts while living, are doomed to always end up on the lower levels. Rachel explained that I was brought up in church to believe in being saved. She said my belief system is on the right track, being saved actually means turning from your wicked ways. It means turning to a life of service to others. It's the realization you have done such horrible things, while waking up to a knowing you want to turn your life around. The realizing you want to live in a way that is not only pleasing to the Creator but pleasing to yourself. She told me you save yourself from the lower levels by doing this.

I asked her why anyone would want to live in a place like this. She explained that although our world has many wonderful qualities, it's also filled with so much greed and hate as well. "Your world is comprised of much self-gratification and earthly pleasures at the expense of hurting others." She said some souls choose that life; that's what they want. "God never intended for anyone to end up on one of the lower levels. But some souls, they choose to be there by their own works." Rachel explained that this lower realm is the place where there is absolutely no hope left for a person at all. I asked if a person living such a horrible life has any chance at all of making amends; could they avoid going to this level. "If a soul comes to the realization that it has committed horrible acts against others and acquires that knowing within. If that soul has any hope at all, even the size of a grain of sand, of the life that should have been lived; if that soul begins to demonstrate that it will change and live for good, then there is hope. For where there is hope there is love. Because of the smallest amount of hope and love, that soul cannot go to the lowest level."

After that conversation with Rachel, I realized just how horrible of an existence those souls that were there had lived. At that point, I asked if that level is what we know as Hell. Rachel nodded her head yes and explained that Hell is a state of evil and suffering, not literal like we're taught. Those that reside there, do so by their own choosing. She reminded me they are given multiple chances to redeem themselves. She stated that God in no way wishes to see any soul endure that suffering. She emphasized again that Hell is a state of mind, and those that create that state of mind, do so while in body form.

The second realm is still not good but definitely better than the first. At this point, I realized why I couldn't see these levels while crossing over. The second level is no piece of cake either I assure you; souls there are tormented by demons as well. This realm does contain some light, but gray and dismal. It's dense and thick, with a feeling of being weighted down. It contained those souls who had also committed horrible acts. The difference in the second level was at least there is some type of hope. Rachel pointed out that God never created these lower levels; man did this to himself by his deeds and actions. Rachel said that nothing bad or evil ever came from God. Because of ungodly actions, there was no choice but to create a manifested place, a state of being, where man could experience the hurt and torment he had inflicted on others.

I saw the second realm as a place where souls who have lived horrible lives go, but, they have demonstrated there is some hope. Souls there still experience misery, pain, torment, etc. This realm is not meant for punishment, it is meant to bring about an awareness of all bad acts committed against others. My observation was the lowest level for a soul is eternal. Eventually after a time, those souls would be reabsorbed back into the source of creation. On the second level, the time there is determined by how soon a soul realizes what it has done. It is determined by how fast the soul feels remorse and shame for acts committed, which leads to an eventual moving up to a higher level.

Rachel explained while there are souls who reside on the second level for hundreds and thousands of years, many souls come to this knowing or realization within a short time. Once they obtain this knowing, they never return to the way they were.

She told me this is where the Universal Law of Grace comes in. It states that once a soul repents of evil ways and comes to the knowing of wrong that has been done, the Law of Grace takes over; that allows the soul to move on. No one need remain on this level. It is up to an individual soul to become aware and move on.

I learned the two lower levels are the most far away from God, or the Source. The lowest realm cannot possibly feel close to the Creator because the Creator is all love, hope, and peace. Those souls there choose to be void of any of these wonderful feelings. How sad that they are there, and even worse, they did it to themselves.

The third realm I encountered is the Borderland. This is where I observed souls that had no idea they had even died (or ceased to exist). We must remember that the soul never dies; only the body dies for the soul is eternal. This level housed souls that were so materialistic during a life they simply had no time for growing closer to the Creator. It's not that they were bad people, just so consumed by earthly possessions and what they could acquire while here. That mentality enveloped their whole being. Because of desire for earthly possessions, they created for themselves a life that tied them down to the Earth and the materialistic side of Earth. It was as if they just wandered aimlessly in the same routine over and over. It reminded me in many ways of the movie "Groundhog Day." I saw many caregivers walking among them. They were trying to bring them into the light of an upper level. I know now that's where we get our term Earthbound Spirits from. Some take longer than others to realize where they're at but eventually they all move on up.

We must remember the life we live here is what we carry over with us when we go. If you lead a pretty good life, you try and do good, help others when you can, etc., you don't have to worry about the lower levels. Rachel stressed several times why it's so important to have balance in our lives. It's fine to make a living and want nice things in life. It's fine to take time to do for yourself, but there has to be balance. Balance means not only making a living but living life and enjoying life. Balance is realizing the joy that can be found in a walk through the woods, or playing with animals. It's being still long enough to listen to what God has to say to you. With that balance comes not only taking time for you but taking time for others as well. It's taking time to teach a child something, or to take a meal to a shut in. Taking time to listen as someone pours their heart out to you because they are hurting. It means being understanding of those who don't think the same as we do. This is balance, and we must achieve that balance here if we want to have it when our time comes to go back home.

I spoke with a man who had crossed over; he explained while living his life on Earth he was a billionaire. He told me he had every luxury you could imagine; he spent millions and billions acquiring those things. He looked down on those less fortunate many times. He felt they had every opportunity he had to create wealth, and wealth was what it was all about for him. He showed me meals in which he paid $500 a plate for food, while others were starving. It's not that he was a bad person, just all about himself. He never married and had children, although he had numerous relationships with women. Many of them he hurt, in order to gain what he wanted. He said that's really all he cared about. He showed me expensive cars and watches; he even had a luxurious yacht with the finest liquors and food you could buy. He never took the time to notice a beautiful sunset or the beauty in the rain.

When his body died, and he first crossed over, he didn't even know he was dead. He said it was like he just woke up one morning on his yacht and couldn't leave for some reason. He could see water but that was all. There was no beach, sun, moon, people, nothing. He said he still had his expensive food and liquor. It was like an endless cycle of eating and getting drunk; he admitted at first it was great. He would sleep night and day, sit on the deck, make himself something to eat, fix a drink, and read a book from his library. After doing that same thing for what seemed like hundreds of times, he began to get agitated with himself. He became lonely, which led to thoughts of family he never had time for. He thought about those who would have been good friends had he only given them a chance. He told me he spent his time reflecting on his life; what he had missed out on all those years.

Eventually, he reached the point of feeling remorse for things he didn't do; times he could have helped people and he didn't. He felt bad for not helping some of the people living on the streets asking for food. He told of how he would snub those people. He thought of the time a young man came to him, asking for a job. He turned him down because of the clothes he was wearing. These thoughts began to fester; it ate at him like a cancer to the point he thought he would go mad. There is no time there, but he estimated in earthly time he spent around twenty-five years alone on that yacht. "It was just me and my material possessions I loved, I couldn't leave," he said.

One day he cried out and asked why this happened to him. He came to realize, because of the life he'd lived on earth, he was living it over and over again. It was during that realization he was met by a caregiver. He told me the man reminded him of someone that lived on the streets by the way he was dressed; this man talked with him. He was so grateful just to have someone to talk with he never once thought bad of him or why he might have been homeless. The man offered him a peanut butter and jelly sandwich. He told me he gladly accepted his offering. He enjoyed that simple sandwich so much; every bite was like a delicacy to him. He realized how much life he had missed out on by not recognizing there is joy in the simplest of things. He said he felt an instant connection to the man. It was at that very moment he finally understood the true meaning of life. With that came the knowing that we are all brothers and sisters. The last thing he said to me was he was going to get it right the next time around.

The next level I saw, was one where souls went that died prematurely by their own hand or by that of someone else. This level is for what I would call trauma victims. Souls were there that had died of murder, drug overdoses, alcohol, suicide, etc. This level contained hospitals and care stations. Many care workers were there that meet souls when they cross over. They take care of them, wrapping them in nothing but pure love; I'm told it's like a type of cocooning. There's no set time for them. These souls are there for as long as it takes to heal from whatever trauma they encountered. Rachel told me that suicide should never be an option. She said when a soul commits suicide, their contract between the soul and the Creator for that particular lifetime, is broken. She said all souls who commit suicide are sent back out into life. The hardships they experienced while here, are sent to them once again in hopes they may learn to better handle life and rely on spiritual helpers. She assured me that God loves them as well as each and every soul.

Chapter Five

My Journey-Part Two

The next level reminded me of my life here; matter of fact, it looked pretty much like my daily surroundings. It appeared to be a realm where souls who cross over go because they're pretty satisfied with their lives. I saw those who represented all walks. These people never missed a beat; it was as if they never stopped living their life on earth. There were buildings much like what is here, along with churches, ball fields, football stadiums, salons, theaters, restaurants, businesses, etc.; every kind of structure filled this level. By all accounts, it reminded me of earthly living. Rachel explained the souls living in this realm are aware they have crossed over; they're just not quite ready to move up to a more spiritual realm. They enjoyed their way of life. They lived it to the fullest for themselves, but also helping others when in need. They weren't selfish people; just ones who savored everything daily living could give. They were free to stay as long as they wished in hopes of one day moving on up.

The next level seemed a little more upper class, more like something out of the big cities. Keep in mind I'm from the country; this level had its beauty but it definitely wasn't country. I saw great buildings like laboratories; they were tall with a shiny metallic hue. It reminded me more of a sterile environment, a no nonsense level. People who looked like scientists, doctors, and researchers were hurrying around. There were many groups of people in discussions, like classrooms. Rachel explained to me that a high percentage of ideas for inventions, scientific research, cure for diseases, etc., come from this realm. She said their ideas are passed down to earth so that those who work in corresponding fields may hopefully use them for good.

I spoke with a scientist there who showed me his latest project. He explained that the Earth's sun has been in the process of serious change for many of Earth's years. He was working on an advanced growing system for vegetation. He explained there would be many environmental changes to come, as well as catastrophic events involving the weather. I was made aware at this point of the "Guardians, or Watchers of Earth." He explained how Earth, in more years past than we can count, evolved to a point where man abused her and cared not what happened. He showed me where our big corporations employ many brilliant scientists who don't always realize how much money and power is gained through their skills. I was told that power always comes at a cost.

This greed for power created problems that lead to natural disasters, failed crops, disease, famine, death, etc. He pointed out that everything we see now upon the Earth, has run in cycles many times before. At that time, God appointed the Guardians to keep an eye on the happenings of Earth. Their main job is downplaying natural disasters. He explained some occurrences are allowed because man has strayed so far away from God; man must endure suffering at his own hand. He mentioned how Karmic debt has to be balanced and the fact that God did not create the mess the Earth is in. It is by man's own hand, he must endure what is to come. I asked if there would be more of these disasters. "Unless man turns from his manipulative and greedy ways, these things will continue until Karmic debt is balanced. If man does not wake up, the cycle will continue."

The next level was the best that I was blessed to see. It contained the Hall of Records and the Viewing Hall. I had the privilege of meeting a member of the Divine Council of Elders there. To me, this was the most fascinating level of all. I felt privileged just to take a tour and view some of the happenings. The first thing I saw was a viewing room; it was large, much like a theater. A soul that crosses over goes in a viewing room to see their present life from birth until the body ceases. I'm told this is a very important step in the process of crossing back over. It's meant to help you be aware of the life you lived and how you lived it. Every second, minute, hour, day, month, and year is shown and accounted for; no detail is ever left out. It was amazing just to watch as the movie of my life played. I'd lived a pretty good life; I loved people and tried to help when I could. I also witnessed scenes in which I could have helped someone in need but didn't. Many times I felt I was too busy, or felt my needs took precedence over theirs. I felt the hurt of those I denied help, those closest to me and others I never knew. Likewise, there were many times I did help. I felt love from even the smallest acts of kindness; acts that never go unrecognized.

In one particular scene, I was in line at the store; there was an elderly lady in front of me paying for her groceries. As her shaking hand counted the money, she realized she was a few dollars short. She told the cashier she would have to put some things back; there were only a few items to begin with. My gut instinct told me to pay for her order, so I did. I felt a strong sense she was really in need. She teared up and thanked me several times while trying to repay me. I told her it was my pleasure; I was so glad I could help. I never knew anything about her situation other than she was short on money.

During my life review, I witnessed events leading up to this precious soul going to the grocery store. She was on a fixed income, very careful in budgeting her money each month. She lived a simple life, no real luxuries, etc. She'd heard that a close friend of hers was very sick. When she visited the friend, she learned the lady was unable to afford her insulin for the month. This dear soul, even though she had little, went to the drug store and paid for the insulin. She did this freely and without hesitation. She'd made out her grocery list for the whole month before the visit. Because she'd helped her friend, her list was cut down to the bare minimum. I realized after seeing that scene, she was able to go again and buy food to finish out the month because I'd paid for her order.

Rachel reminded me of an evening when Guerry and I had gone to eat at a nearby restaurant. Our meal, tip and all, was about $35.00. "Are you aware the amount you spent on that one meal out would pay for that dear soul's groceries for half the month?" she asked. I can promise you it was one of the most humbling experiences I've ever had. I realized at that very moment, just how much in life we take for granted. I'd always had a heart for those in need; after that, the desire to help grew even more.

I saw many books in the Great Hall of Records. Shelves were lined with volumes that looked hundreds and thousands of years old. These books were leather bound and oversized; each one displayed a name. I was so fascinated I stopped for a moment just to inhale the smell of eternity. I wanted to bask in the greatness of these remarkable creations. Rachel explained these books contained the many lifetimes of all souls who were ever created. Every second, minute, hour, day, year, and month, in earthly time, was recorded on their massive pages. She explained that as Christians, we believe in the Book of Life; in reality, there are many Books containing all lives.

She pointed out my book; when I touched it I felt an intense energy and connection with it. I admit I was a bit confused by the name on the label. It was familiar to me but my brain seemed fuzzy. Rachel explained each soul is honored with a name given by the Creator; that name remains always with that soul. When we are born, our parents give us an earthly name, but the soul always retains its creation name. I was told when people cross over they know each other by recognizing the soul.

It was then I learned about the meaning of soul groups. Rachel explained when souls were first created zillions (that's my word) of years ago, they were placed in groups of usually around twenty to thirty souls. These groups are known as soul groups. They've always traveled together and continue to do so to learn lessons they need to know. Rachel asked if I'd ever met someone I had an instant connection with; someone I didn't know, yet felt I did. The souls we're closest to back home are the ones we recognize first, even though we may not know them here. I think she really picked up on my confusion. She took me by the hand and led me back to the viewing room. What I saw next completely changed my life forever.

There were three screens in this part of the viewing hall; each began to play clips. I saw movies in which my soul participated in different lives. I watched on one screen as my soul had a life in Bangladesh. In this life, I helped run an orphanage and cared for many children on the streets. Those children lived in poverty; my heart broke for them. All I had to give them was love and a little food; those children were my passion, I would have given my life for them. I watched as a group of men ransacked the village. They took what little food the orphanage had; the children were killed. I was locked into a basement closet with two babies for protection, by the dear priest who lived there. When he was killed, no one was left to unlock the closet; no one ever knew we were there. Nobody came, we were left to die. "Because of this experience, today you are Claustrophobic," Rachel said. "You abhor thoughts of being confined in a tight space. You are also very protective of children and you don't always trust people. Sometimes events in past lives carry over; they filter through." This made me instantly think of a man I worked for years ago. From the first time I met him, I felt I had known him forever; we had an instant connection. He was so kind to me, took me under his wing so to speak, to teach me the job. He even said on a couple of different occasions, he felt he had always known me. I recognized his soul as being the priest there at the orphanage.

On another screen, I saw where I had a wonderful life in Ireland. I was a healer and lived in a castle on the outskirts of the village. My sons today lived that life with me there; they were my protectors. My daughter and daughter in law lived in the castle as well; they were both apprentices to healing. My sons spent countless hours safeguarding me in that lifetime, riding alongside when I would travel throughout the lands helping people. The girls would run the castle when I was gone, organizing and helping those in need; they were sisters then. At times they adored each other, other times they fought like cats and dogs. My boys were strong in that lifetime, great warriors; today they still retain those same traits. They would do anything to protect their families. Both are old school, where your handshake is your word. They're strong, and many times I've laughed and said they remind me of great warriors. The girls, let's just say they are both OCD, have to be organized, and work together in the same office helping loads of people each week. They still get irritated with each other, but are the best of friends, more like sisters than anything.

Even more amazing is in 2007, my husband and I took a trip to Ireland with his Mother and her husband. When we landed I felt a surge go through my feet the minute we stepped off the plane. I looked at my husband and said, "You know, for some reason I feel like I'm home." To this day I still feel such a calling to return there at times. Both my sons have expressed an interest in visiting Ireland, Scotland, etc. If you take a tour of my house, you'll find my herb room where I mix and make salves, potions, tinctures, etc., all for helping my family and others. When I'm watching TV and see a show about Ireland, I light up; it's like a craving my soul has to go back. If I'm tired, I can play some Irish music for a few minutes and it's almost healing to me.

A few weeks ago my Granddaughters and I were watching TV. I was scrolling through channels when I came across the most beautiful scenes of Ireland, accompanied by Irish music. My three year old Granddaughter stopped dead in her tracks, walked up to the TV, and just stood there watching the vivid, almost breathtaking scenes that were displayed. We have a 70 inch TV, so it honestly feels like you're right there in the picture.

She was absolutely mesmerized. When it was over she asked if I would play it again. When I told her it had gone off, she looked at me so sad and said, "Granmama I love that, I want to see it again." The next time she came to visit about a week later, she asked me if we could watch that show again. Pay attention to those little ones around you; their interests provide many clues to past experiences.

On the next screen, I witnessed a life in which I was never married. I came from money; I spent my days reading, writing, and playing various musical instruments. My days there could only be described as carefree. It's so amazing that although I'm such a social butterfly here today, I still crave that time alone; it's how I recharge my batteries. I love to get by myself with a good book, or play my piano because it's such a passion of mine.

After seeing all these clips, life really began to make sense. It was as if the pieces of the puzzle were being brought together. I learned that sometimes when we go places we've never been before it causes us to have that "deja vu" moment. For a split second, the thought crosses that we've been there. It's no coincidence; most likely it's because we have, just maybe not in this lifetime. I was told the things we are the most passionate about in life now, are things we've most likely experienced many times before.

I had a lady come by my house one day to pick up some salve. She told me that for years she'd dreamed of opening up a little bakery in a small town somewhere; she felt such a passion for doing this. She described every detail of the building to me, the equipment she would have in it, and how she would run the business down to the many delicacies she would create and serve. Now I've been a baker for years. This woman rattled off techniques, ingredients, and combinations she felt would make recipes better. I thought after talking with her that she'd owned a bakery somewhere before. She was just so knowledgeable of the business. I sat with my mouth gaped open when she told me she knew nothing about it. Matter of fact, she didn't even bake or cook much. I'll let you draw your own conclusions on that one, but I have no doubt it was filtering through from another experience she'd had.

At this point, I realize some of you are shaking your heads and saying, "No way!" You're asking how this is possible. Parts of this story go against many of our teachings, especially here in the South. One of the Divine Elders told me I would encounter this and offered his advice. He explained I should in no way feel harsh at my upbringing or teachings. He said in my area, this is the way children are taught. He told me that it is up to each individual person as they age in life, to find their way. "Always appreciate your religious roots for they have paved the way. It is time now, to add to them," he said. Before we ever come here we make a pact with God; he explained it very well.

"You are sent to earth to learn lessons. When the Creator first made everything many eons ago, it was due to a desire in which to learn. Through these new souls that were created (God's Children), the Creator would be able to experience life on every possible level. In your Bible, Genesis 1:26 tells us "Let us make man in OUR image, in OUR likeness, so that THEY may rule over the fish in the sea and the birds in the sky, over the livestock and all the wild animals, and over the creatures that move along the ground." One must remember that your Bible was inspired by God (infallible) but written by man (fallible)." It was then I learned about the female side of God. I could never once recall learning about a "Motherly" side of God as in "Our image."

"Much of God's word was omitted or changed because the rulers of that day decided they wanted the Creator's words to benefit them, and their agenda. Greed and power was present then as well my child; it is nothing new to us. Man included just what he wanted to include in the words you now read." I was speechless, mad, and sad, all at once. "There are many Lost, Forgotten books, and Ancient Sacred Texts. Would you be familiar with any of these by chance?" he asked. At the time of our conversation I was not; I assure you I've studied them in depth since, and they are fascinating.

In a lot of ways I'm so grateful for my upbringing and what I was taught. In many ways I'm sad as well, that so much was omitted from our teachings, important things that should have been learned from the very beginning. It's not my Parents or Grandparents fault, they didn't know either. They taught me from what they knew. I learned that in other parts of the world, these teachings are standard but in some religious sects, not so much. The Divine Council Elder then assured me, there is no way we can possibly learn everything we need to learn, in one life time; it's just not going to happen. This brought us back to the Hall of Records where all accounts of lives are kept and stored. He asked if I would like to sit in on a planning session. "Are you kidding?" I could hardly contain the anticipation.

I strolled along with him to a room in the Great Hall; it was huge, with an almost endless ceiling. A great stone lion was on each side of the entrance. It was lined with massive tables and books as well. The shelves were filled from top to bottom; it reminded me of a great library. The furniture was so exquisite. It was magnificent and the craftsmanship was like no other I'd ever seen. It was like mahogany or some gorgeous wood; it appeared to be hand carved. I could see figures on the chairs; they were upholstered with something similar to dark red velvet. The carvings were of different animals, men and women dressed like warriors, the sun, moon, stars, etc. It was like looking through the eyes of creation.

The chairs surrounded a great oval table with legs so massive. Each one looked as if it could withstand hundreds of pounds in weight. The great double doors were guarded by an angel on each side. Those two angels were massive as well; they had to have been at least 10 feet tall or more, with broad shoulders. They were very stately but yet so peaceful. When time came for the session to begin, men and women in white robes were escorted in to sit around the table. I counted thirteen but was told there are many. Rachel was with me; she explained this was one of many Divine Councils of Elders. She said they are wise beings that God created from the very beginning. She also explained how we say God, but they address as Creator or Yahweh. She explained how Yahweh, because of a desire to never be alone, created helpers in the form of Council members, Angels, watchers, guardians, guides, etc.

Each member sat in silence for a moment, as if giving reverence to the one who presides over all. Rachel explained that even though Yahweh created these helpers to rule with Him, He is still the one, true, original God; the only one that knows everything that has always been, is now, and always will be. The angels then escorted a soul into the room; that soul stood before the Council. Even though I could not see God/Yahweh physically present there, I knew that presence was everywhere.

I'd like to point out something to you before I go any farther. It's very difficult to tell this story and use the terms he or she. When a soul is home and just in soul form, it's non gender. The only time a soul is referred to as he or she is when it's in earthy form as a man or a woman. If I describe a soul as he or she, it's because that was their form in their most recent life. Rachel said this particular soul had recently crossed back over and had completed the life review. At this point, all I felt from the council was pure love and empathy; it was a very sacred meeting.

The Elder who escorted me through the Great Hall greeted the soul and asked if it was beginning to get re accustomed to the surroundings; yes was the answer. "Good, it does us well to hear of that." The same Elder began by asking if it had learned any lessons during the lifetime on Earth. The soul answered by saying it felt like it had learned how to be more compassionate toward others, but not as compassionate as it could have been in many situations. Another council elder asked if the soul would explain.

"There were many times I noticed during my life review, where help could have been given to others but the choice was made not to. I never thought of myself as being selfish while living but realized after the life review, just how selfish of a life I had lived. Often I could have helped someone but chose not to." The council elder asked why he felt he could not take the time to help those in need? "When I watched my life through the years, I found that I was just so busy; I didn't take the time to notice others. I was so consumed with making a living, taking care of my house and family, and being a part of life." The council asked if any one situation stood out in particular.

"Once I met a man on the street, asking for work in order to buy food. I stared at him sitting there with that homemade sign of his. I thought to myself, he doesn't need help. He's just sitting on the ground; he should be out working a job like I do. It was a cold and breezy day. He had a blanket over him and a cap on. I drove right by him that day and did nothing." The council asked why this particular situation stood out. "During my life review, I saw that he sat there for almost ten hours on that cold day. When he got ready to leave and removed the blanket, he only had one leg. That leg was not in good shape; it was somewhat crippled. I realized he was diabetic, born that way. He had a sore on his foot as well, that wouldn't heal. I felt his pain during my life review to the point it made me feel sick. Then I read the sign again the man was holding and the words made me tear up. He wasn't asking for a handout, he was asking for work so that he might feed himself. I felt the feeling of judgement I had on him and it made me feel like a horrible person. I saw where only one person stopped that day out of several hundred that drove right by. That man went home to a cold house with a loaf of bread and a jar of peanut butter, bought with money that person gave him. He was very grateful for it. That same night, my family and I had a high dollar steak dinner and movie night out."

I could see and feel the hurt in his eyes, the hurt from passing the man by. One of the Elders posed a question; he asked if by earthly standards the man considered himself to have been pretty fortunate and blessed. He nodded his head yes. "May we ask why you did not feel the need to help the man that day? Have you learned anything from this experience?" He began to cry, as he told the council he now realized how he passed judgement on others during his life. He realized he had no right to judge anyone, for most of the time he never even knew their situation. He said he saw people he could have helped but never made the effort because of judgement. After that, one of the elders made a statement. "It appears to us that you are very sincere and you feel you have learned from your lessons in this lifetime while on earth. If you choose to learn more lessons, would you decide to live a somewhat diffcrent life?

This man told the council that he wanted only to live a life of service, one in which he could help others. He wanted to make up for all the things he didn't do, by living a productive life. It was his desire to make a difference, instead of just working and earning a living. He was told they were very proud of what he had learned and he would have help planning his next life, if he chose, from his Guides and Angels; he was told to go in peace.

Rachel asked if I'd seen enough, but no, I wanted to stay. "As you wish," she said. The next meeting was that of a lady who'd lived a very glamorous life. She'd been a beauty queen many times, beginning with middle school years. During her life review she'd witnessed on many occasions her bad treatment of others, especially women. Her reputation was that of being a stuck up rich snob. She didn't mind at all being labeled with that; in fact she loved it, because that was her life. She could never imagine herself being any other way. She enjoyed being spoiled each day; she didn't have to care what others thought.

During her life review, she'd seen how her cruelty of others impacted them. She didn't care what anyone thought of her; she came from money. She could have pretty much anything she wanted. In her climb up the beauty ladder, she witnessed many times where she made other women feel so beneath her. One scene in particular, she talked about; she choked back tears while telling of it.

"I was a freshman in high school. The weeks leading up to pageant time were filled with excitement. There was a fellow student that walked with crutches, because of a deformed foot. I'd seen her around school most days but never talked to her. She was beautiful; everyone always talked about how sweet she was, how she had such a good heart. It made me sick to my stomach to hear them say that. Everybody loved her, but I was jealous. She had a natural beauty about her, whereas I had to work for mine. I overheard her talking about being in the pageant. She said she didn't expect to win. She just wanted to know the thrill of competing, so she entered.

Students around her, including some of my friends, began to lend their support. I was so angry and afraid that she would win. I was jealous of her. That jealousy ate at me to a point where I couldn't even stand to look at her when she passed me in the hall. The morning of the pageant, I knew she would be singing. I'd heard her sing in chorus, she'd done several solos; she had a beautiful voice. As she walked out on stage to practice, I tripped her as she passed through the curtain. She fell so hard she cut her face, blood went everywhere. To make it worse, I laughed about it backstage while others ran out to help her. When I saw how much blood there was, as she was getting up, I did feel a little bad about it. I didn't really mean for her to get hurt; I just wanted to embarrass her. She didn't even compete that evening. I won that day, but I really won nothing at all. I sacrificed everything to hurt someone that was innocent, all because of vanity."

Again, I could feel the sickness that lady felt by the way she treated her school mate. There were many more similar scenarios throughout her entire life. Scenes that made her feel such compassion for those lives she'd affected. I learned a great lesson that day. Some souls feel so much remorse for their treatment of others; they feel they have to make serious amends for it. After much discussion, she explained she wanted to have the chance to live a life in which she was crippled; she wanted to be like the girl she had hurt. She wanted to experience her life and how she felt when treated badly. I couldn't believe what I was hearing. I asked Rachel why she would choose this; she explained in depth about Karma and Karmic debt.

Oh it's very real folks and it does catch up with us; no one is immune from it. I saw firsthand why it's so important to make amends while here, for things we've done to hurt others. How can you do this you may ask? When you come to that realization you've done things less than desirable, make a pact with yourself that you'll begin anew. Try following the Golden Rule which says, "Do unto others as you would have them do unto you." Do a self-check. Are you fair in your treatment of others? If not, it's never too late to change. Do you treat those around you with love and respect? Are you compassionate with your fellow man, even though you may not understand his or her lifestyle? Do you live a life free of judgement? We must remember our path is not to judge, it is to help and be of service to those who need us; our path is simply to love.

Chapter Six

My Journey-Part Three

Guerry and I recently watched a show on Netflix called the Returned. It's about people who've come back from the dead for whatever reason. Hey, remember it happened to Lazarus, so who are we to question. One little boy in particular, called Victor, was murdered alongside his mom in a robbery of their house. Years later he comes back. At first he has no idea who he is, he's just going through the motions. He doesn't even speak; people take him in and care for him. All of a sudden his memory starts to come back when he meets a man who is a fine, upstanding citizen of the community. This man has devoted his adult life to doing only good things and helping others. He runs a little village of sort, for those in need who have nowhere to go. You would have thought this man was a saint at first.

One day Victor hears the man say something; it triggers a memory with him. Victor realizes the man was one of two men, who robbed and killed his mother and him. He eventually tells him that he knows who he is. Victor says, "You killed me and my mom." The man is so stunned; he stares at him and it's like a lightbulb goes off. He looks into his eyes and remembers. He takes Victor out to the cemetery and shows him the grave of his friend, the friend who was with him the day of the robbery. He explains to Victor that they were young and stupid. The friend had talked him into robbing the house, because they thought no one was home.

He pours his heart out in an attempt to explain how everything went awry. He wasn't the one who shot them; it was his friend who did it. It ate at him so bad; he vowed to be of service to others, so he might somehow make amends for what had happened. He asked Victor to forgive him. It was clear this man was so sad for what had happened and it changed him.

When I saw that episode, it reminded me of things I'd witnessed on the Other Side. It's not hard; it's really very simple. We all mess up and do things we shouldn't. The difference being when our actions hurt people, it brings about a whole different ballgame. It's never too late to change that, when we realize the wrong we've done to others. Some people choose to be born with a birth defect. Others choose to be born with mental issues. Others choose to be born with physical or mental hindrances. Many times that reason is to satisfy Karmic Debt. Again, this is from my point of observation while there. It does get a little more complicated but I'll try my best to explain.

Sometimes, because of losing their way and past treatment of others, souls choose to experience tough situations. They do this to satisfy their karmic debt. Now we haven't said a lot about Karmic debt, so now is probably a good time to explain again what that is. If you choose to google Karma, you will probably notice it may fall under Hinduism or Buddhism. I assure you with every fiber of my being, Karma is in no way specific of just those religions. It is universal and worldwide; yep it's everywhere folks. There is absolutely and positively, no way on Earth or anywhere else, you can run from Karma. Maybe we should discuss it a little more.

Karma was never supposed to be about payback, just learning lessons. Our actions, every action we choose to perform, does and will have consequences. One definition of Karma is an invisible force that teaches you lessons you need to learn. Every thought you have, every action you perform, carries with it a type of energy. Whenever you think a thought (whether good or bad), or do something (whether good or bad), that energy flows out into the universe. This is where the phrase "An Eye for an Eye" comes from. One guide showed me the Seven Levels of Karmic Debt that is recognized by the Universe. I was told that our present day Earth, especially America, is experiencing level six the most. I won't go into detail about all the levels here; I'll save that info for my second book. I'll just say it involves government and world leaders keeping people in the dark, influencing them in less than desirable ways. I'm told it's really going to come back around and hit them hard.

The best way to sum this up is, "whatever you do, whether good or not good, will always come back to you." So by now, I'm sure some of you are anxious to google Karma, especially if you're not familiar with it. Go ahead; it will probably pop up telling you it's a Buddhist term. Again, I cannot stress enough that it is not exclusive of Buddhism or any other ism. It's a universal term, a word that means you better watch what you do and practice good deeds. If you don't, the bad deeds are coming back to bite you on the butt. I read a good explanation of Karma. "When birds are alive, they eat ants. When the birds die, the ants eat the birds. One tree makes a million matchsticks. Only one matchstick is needed to burn down a million trees. You may be powerful now, but your circumstances can change." Karma is powerful. Don't hurt anyone; be good and do good. It's not really all that hard folks.

I spoke with a lady one day and bless her heart, she was going through a really difficult time. Within the first fifteen minutes she'd already bashed several family members, especially one cousin in particular. It was as plain as the nose on her face she was very jealous of this lady. Matter of fact, she spent practically a whole hour talking trash about her cousin. During this conversation she brought up her health problems which included sleepless nights, restless legs, and chronic headaches. Sometime during our talk, I may have mentioned how we reap what we sow; this rule applies not only to actions, but thoughts as well. Our treatment of others always comes back to us, often times manifesting as health problems.

You could've heard a pin drop. She stared at me for a moment and said, "I'm a good person; I don't hurt people. I give to the Ronald McDonald House and also St. Jude's. I go to church every time the doors are open and I teach Sunday School." Well now, you that know me well can only imagine what was going through my head. So, I said, "Let me ask you a question? How many hours a day do you spend angry at your cousin?" You could really hear that pin drop then. Now here's the deal. Believe it or not, you can be an outstanding citizen of the community, church leader, member of the city council, and Grand Marshall of the town parade. I'm here to tell you now, that if you harbor resentment, anger, and hatred toward your fellow man, then you've got a problem.

Keep in mind I'm not talking about your occasional little tiff with someone, or that fleeting moment of jealousy. I'm talking about the twenty five year grudge you're holding against your cousin because she got your Grandmother's set of china when she passed instead of you. Folks, after a while guess what's going to happen? That anger, resentment, and jealousy will fester. And where is it going to fester? That's right; it's going to smack you right in the face and cause you some serious health problems. So you see; we've all got to strive to get rid of those grudges. Get rid of the jealousy. Get rid of the anger against our fellowman, or cousin in this instance. Believe me, here in the South we love everybody. We don't like everybody, but we love em. Sometimes that love is hard to do, especially when you think you've been wronged, and especially when your cousin got the china you always wanted.

So in summing all this up, we come to this conclusion. Sometimes, if a soul has done some horrible things within a lifetime, I mean things that would eat at your very core, then that soul will purposely choose a hard life. They may choose a life similar to the person or persons they have hurt the most. That very often includes a life of being severely mistreated, sick, or abused, etc. When a soul does this, it's because they want to satisfy their Karmic debt a whole lot faster. This little story may help a bit for those of you who are feeling faint or your head is spinning.

I have an acquaintance that was having some real issues. I suggested due to the severity of her issues she seek out a past life regressionist. She'd been dealing with severe psoriasis and frequent outbreaks of hives. She'd been to every doctor in the tri state area and prescribed several medications that absolutely did no good whatsoever. She'd taken herbal supplements, drank herbal teas, tried every prescription cream and lotion on the market, as well as all natural; nothing helped. She was miserable; she'd been this way for over thirty years. She claimed the psoriasis was so painful, that her skin burned like fire. She could hardly walk because it was so bad on the soles of her feet. I asked her to keep me updated about what happened; she gave me permission to tell you.

After her past life regression, the therapist explained how she talked in great detail about living during the Middle Ages. It was a time when torture was used frequently and she described various torture techniques which I will not go into detail about here. She spoke of being a man in that life who hurt people in the castle torture chamber. She said she was good at several different types of torture, but her specialty was burning people. She particularly enjoyed burning the soles of the feet, arms, and face. Often times she would even burn the hair off of someone. Here is an excerpt from her email to me and it's very direct.

"I'm so thankful for your suggestion that I have a past life regression. I've listened to the tape of my session dozens of times and I continue to be amazed. Some of the things I described left me shaking my head in such disgust and horror. But the most profound point is when I talked of burning victims on the soles of their feet, arms, face, and hair. When I heard myself describe this on the tape, it sent chills up my spine for those are the exact places on my body where the psoriasis is. I'm thankful to report though, that after my regression session, my psoriasis is now miraculously healing up." Wow! I might be wrong but it sure does sound a lot like satisfying Karmic debt doesn't it? You might ask why after the session it begins to heal? It's because in this life, she comes to the realization of how horrible her actions were in a previous life.

Now with that being said, I also want to point out that's not always the case. Not everyone born with a birth defect is trying to satisfy Karmic Debt. Not everyone who is murdered, or comes down with a dreaded disease, is trying to satisfy karma. I state again *sometimes,* that is the case. To be perfectly honest, I have no idea how everything works in our vast universe. I only know, as I said before, we are not meant to understand it all. Only the Creator God can possibly know everything there is to know; God/Yahweh is the one and only original. The Bible is correct in saying that not even the angels in heaven know some things, for they don't.

After meeting with the elders, I was escorted into a life planning session. I just thought what I'd seen before was amazing, but believe me, it just got better and better. I was among those in a room who were part of a soul group. It was like being in a classroom with a dry erase board up front. Now keep in mind, when you are on the Other Side you can take whatever form you'd like. It doesn't matter how you choose to look because everyone knows you by your soul energy. I did observe, whenever souls meet in groups, they tend to take the form of one of their favorite lives. This particular group had about 20 members who were present. Now the big question is this; you can bet I asked it too. How can you be on the Other Side and be living another life at the same time?

This planning session consisted of souls who constantly travel together throughout lives helping one another. There were two guides, or planners present at a table. It sort of reminded me of just a regular meeting with two people who were in charge. Rachel and I sat in the back and watched, as one of the guides explained to me how all this works.

"Think of yourself, each soul, as a pie with let's say 12 different slices." Now it's going to get a little complicated here again. By now, I think you can see why it's not been the easiest task to write this book. When I said I had tons of information, I wasn't kidding. "Everyone has several lives at one time going on in different places. This first slice or life, maybe you are a doctor in California, a brain surgeon. You're famous, helping people 24/7. The next slice, you're a teacher in Brazil. The next slice, you may be a beggar on the streets of Chicago. Okay, let's stop with three slices. In the first one where you are the doctor, you're living a life to learn certain lessons. In this life, some of the members of your soul group have agreed to help you learn those lessons. In Brazil where you are the teacher, you are only there to help a couple of people in your soul group who are living lives as students; that one is sort of a low key life. You agreed from the beginning, to be their teacher at some point to help them along their way. In the next life, where you are a beggar on the streets, you chose it because you are trying to satisfy Karmic debt; you're doing this because of how you treated people in the past." By this time my brain was spinning in a hundred different directions.

"Souls who choose the hardest of lives, are known as the warrior souls. They are counseled and guided well. It is sometimes suggested they not try and tackle too much at once because it may be too difficult. If they choose to do so, it's totally up to them. They always have help from the other side, but they must endure those lives because it's what they signed up for. It's like you on Earth, as parents with your children. You love them unconditionally, but sometimes they make bad decisions in spite of your warning and guiding them in other directions. When they do this, often times they must pay the price for wrong things they have done. Do you stop loving them because of the bad decisions? Certainly not, but many times there is simply nothing you can do but let them learn the hard way. It works the same way here." –Guardian Angel Rachel-

I'm told that's what happens sometimes in cases of suicide. A soul makes it too difficult by taking on too much, in spite of being warned. Because of this, they just can't handle life. These slices of pie, they are percentages of your soul; each slice represents a percentage. There must always remain a percentage of the soul, or slice of pie, back home on the Other Side; it's the rule. The guide showed me the pie plate. He pointed out that the entire soul can never ever be gone all at once.

So at this point, I asked the million dollar question? Why when I was growing up, was I taught that we only live one life? The guide asked if he could explain with the help of others in the planning session. "For many years, thousands of years, Christians have been taught to believe that when a person dies, their corpse is buried in the ground. You are taught that a soul sleeps and waits until the final judgement. You believe that on the final day of judgement, all corpses will rise from the graves. This is known as the resurrection. It comes from a misguided teaching in which the words of the Bible were misunderstood. Only the body dies, not the soul. The soul leaves the body as soon as it ceases to exist. Sometimes in very traumatic situations, the soul exits before the body dies. That's what happens, especially in elderly people who seem to just hang on at the end of their life. You watch that body lying there in the hospice setting. They do not speak or open their eyes; they do not eat or drink. If their eyes are open, it is only a fixed stare. This happens when the soul has already gone with only the body left. The shallow breathing is that of the body; the faint pulse is that of the body."

The guide explained to me about reincarnation; it means the rebirth of the soul into a new body and it is as old as time. Because of religious conflicts, teachings being added or left out, reincarnation was made to be a taboo word with Christians. "You must understand there have been many misguided teachings through the ages. Many of these stemmed from fear, with rulers wanting their people to fear them. In 70 AD, there was a struggle between the church that Paul established in Rome and what was left of the Church of Jerusalem that fled to Egypt. There was a conflict between Roman beliefs and Jerusalem beliefs; the Romans won the battle. There are many ancient records of the Pharisees being believers and knowing about reincarnation. As a matter of fact, the Pharisees had it right when they wrote about how the souls of evil men punish themselves and the souls of good men go on to have the power to live again and again."

This is not new stuff I've just made up folks. The other day when I was reading, I came across almost these exact same words. People know this stuff, especially ones growing up in areas that teach it. I, on the other hand had no concept of this; it was new to me. Do you have any idea how difficult it is to write about something that goes totally against some of your teachings? I'm telling you that if not for my NDE, I would still have been in the box with my blinders on.

By now my head was really spinning, yep it was doing a total 360. I must admit my curiosity got the best of me; I listened intently to what I was being taught. It was like being a part of the greatest history class on earth. I was shown scenes of when Jesus walked the earth. People asked Jesus if John the Baptist was the reincarnation of Elijah; He said that yes he was. I've had people to tell me they don't believe it and that's fine. Again, I'm not asking for you to believe me. Pray about it, do your research on the subject. You'll be surprised what you find out. The guide told me that there were ancient teachings of old that were not always made known for fear of persecution.

The rulers back in the old days did not want their people to know about the way things really worked. They wanted to suppress the people and in order to do this, they had to eliminate and forbid certain teachings. This is what happened in relation to reincarnation. I was told we must go back to the original teachings of Jesus; when He walked upon the earth. Jesus taught reincarnation folks. He told others about it and made no bones about doing so. It was even recorded in ancient teachings where two disciples, Origen and Alexandria, wrote about secret teachings being handed down from the apostles, teachings about reincarnation. We all know when Jesus walked the earth there were those that were jealous of His ministry here. There were those that sought only to harm Him and stop Him, because they did not want His teachings known; it was a time of suppression. This is why you only find a few references to it in the Bible.

The guide showed me that back in old times there were ancient mystery schools where those that wished to learn, were taught the secrets of the afterlife. In 553 AD, the teachings of Jesus had to be done in secret. Any teachings, including those about reincarnation and healing, were declared heresy. Not by God, or by Jesus, but by the rulers of that day. The rulers that were scared they would lose control of their people. This so called heresy was made known at that time by the Roman Church. Because of this declaration, an order was given for certain manuscripts and scrolls to be destroyed. A declaration was also made that anyone who talked of these teachings, anyone who attempted to practice any of these teachings, would be put to death. Again, this is a perfect example of God's true words being suppressed. Can you imagine how different our world may have been today if God's word had not been changed by man? What would it be like if we only followed God's true teachings and had only love for our fellowman? What if there was no judgement, no malice, or hate?

Even though the people were scared to death, sacred teachings did not completely stop. There were those brave souls that still taught and learned under the blanket of secrecy. Little did the church know but some of the scrolls that contained the original teachings were carted away in secrecy and saved. They were taken to Upper Egypt where they continued to be taught and eventually buried there; in 1945, some of these secret writings were found. They had been undisturbed for two thousand years. These are some of the most important writings and teachings that have ever been found.

Years later, when I began to do my own research on these teachings, it was amazing what I uncovered. I encourage you to dig into this subject, it's fascinating. The guide told me at this point, reincarnation and the other secret teachings of Jesus had been suppressed for far too long. He said the people of earth are experiencing a great spiritual reawakening, one in which they will begin to know the truth. He said people must wake up and know the truths that have been suppressed, truths that are vital to us as a people; we must wake up and realize the hand of deceit.

He also stated that women were suppressed in the Bible as well. He said the cruel treatment of women must stop. He stated when God created the universe and everything in it, the creation act was brought forth through co- creators, not as separate. Men and women were created in the Creator's image to rule over the lands, not each other. He told me that women are becoming stronger than ever. They are waking up to realize that their days of suppression and mistreatment are rapidly closing.

I was told there would be those who would argue about John being the reincarnation of Elijah. The guide explained that when a person reincarnates, past memories of being someone else and a past life, are blocked out. This is done so they may have a fresh chance to learn new lessons. That's why when some asked John if he was Elijah reincarnated, he stated that he was not. He said at that point he did not realize he had once been Elijah, but Jesus knew better. When Jesus was asked the same question, this is what he said about John the Baptist being Elijah reincarnated. This is Jesus words, "This is the one … there has not risen anyone greater than John the Baptist … And if you are willing to accept it, he is Elijah who was to come. He who has ears let him hear," Matthew 11:11-15.

I was shown that when people reincarnate, they do carry over personality traits with them to other lives. There are great similarities between John the Baptist and Elijah; conscious memories are not carried over but personality traits are. There are many people who have talked about past lives and reincarnation under hypnosis. This is how we explain the little child born and at the age of two, can play a masterpiece on the piano. It's clear this child carried over personality traits of being a great pianist. This is how we explain the child who at the age of four, begins talking about flying airplanes; he loves airplanes so much that all he wants to do is watch them fly. That's because he was a pilot in another life and so forth and so on.

The guide then pointed out something astounding to me. He showed me the prophet Elijah and how he had the priests of Baal brought; they were all killed by the sword. This is the verse in the Bible that tells of this, "Then Elijah commanded them, Seize the Prophets of Baal. Don't let anyone get away! They seized them and Elijah had them brought down to the Kishon Valley and slaughtered there," 1 Kings 18:40. Also 1 Kings 19:1 tells us, "Now Ahab told Jezebel everything Elijah had done and how he had killed all the prophets with the sword." Here is the amazing part. I was made aware of how John the Baptist, who was the reincarnation of Elijah, perished; he was beheaded. I stood there and studied that screen. I couldn't believe what I was being shown. Wow! It was Karma at work; it was the perfect example of paying back Karmic debt.

There are universal laws that must be abided by. "We reap what we sow" and "an eye for an eye;" what you do, comes back around. If it doesn't get you in your present lifetime, it will get you in another. The guide told me that the concept of reincarnation was just common knowledge in the days when Jesus walked the earth. He taught it wherever he went and never reputed it one time. The guide explained that God is a just and righteous God; He is always fair in all ways. He explained that all men and women are given a chance to know life in many different situations and settings, according to the lessons they need to learn. Each one of us has experienced many different life settings. Some people have experienced so many, it's almost like they just know everything. Again, these are the oldest souls.

In some lives we've been poor, some rich, some sick, some healthy, some we are married with children, still others we can have no children. We are all given the chance for fair and equal treatment and learning, but it is up to us what we choose to learn. This is the universal law of free choice and free will. God gives us that gift because nothing, not even learning lessons, is ever forced upon us. Lessons are for the advancement of the soul. There are some who simply choose not to learn at the same rate as others. I saw where the souls who choose to live the most lives and learn the greatest lessons, are the ones who advance at a more rapid pace. These souls are the ones who grow closer to the source, back to God where it all began.

This brings me to the last point here. Sometimes you have souls that live lifetimes where something just goes haywire. I was not told why, just told it does happen. When certain souls began incarnating and reincarnating many thousands and millions of years ago, at times, something just didn't click. You might say a flaw between the soul, the body, and the brain; something just didn't mesh right. When this happened, and it still does, things go crazy; the result is people who become psychotic. They are the serial killers, among other things, etc. They do nothing but inflict pain and torment on those who do not deserve it, on those who are innocent. When they take it upon themselves to commit these heinous crimes to hurt others and it continues, they become the lost souls. These are the souls that cross over to the lowest level. There they will feel every ounce of torment they have inflicted on anyone they have ever hurt. This is where the Christian concept of becoming saved comes from. I really feel the Other Side covered this in so much detail because they want us to know, that God does not desire for anyone to go to the lowest level.

These souls are given every opportunity to turn from their wicked ways; they are given multiple chances to change. I saw again where most of these souls begin, after a time of suffering, to show remorse for what they have done. Eventually they began to take a new direction. After much counseling, many more lives lived, and lessons learned, they move out of that area. Sadly, there are some that never learn; they have no desire whatsoever to change. When they reincarnate, they commit the same atrocities over and over; they continue to inflict hurt and pain.

When the Creator has done everything in its power to give those souls every opportunity there is to take a new direction and those souls continue a life of misery, there is no choice but to cross to the lowest level. When a soul is there, it will feel all the pain and suffering it has ever inflicted on anyone ever hurt. That pain and hurt will be magnified to a point of being tormented so much, that it cries out only wishing to die. But it doesn't die, it can't die; it just keeps reliving the nightmares of hurt and anguish it brought on others as well as itself. At that point I had tears flowing, for in my mind I could never have imagined something so terrible; no wonder it's such a horrible place.

Chapter Seven

A Tough Decision

My final time with Rachel was spent in a beautiful garden. Some of the most gorgeous and exquisite flowers I'd ever seen lined the cobblestone walkways. There were caretakers there, souls who loved working in nature. I was still wrestling with what I'd seen and witnessed. Parts were so amazing, yet troubling as well because of being misled my whole life. Could my existence today be different had I only known the truth? We talked about the caring spiritual beings that assist us on a daily basis. I was blessed enough to witness the arrival of souls coming back home; what a joyous occasion it was. When our bodies cease to exist, when the body dies and the soul comes home, it's like stepping through one doorway and into another. Most of us don't miss a beat; we just continue on with what we need to do.

I know for some of you it's hard to understand that, but the Other Side is simply a continuation of what we do here. That's why there are different levels, with the ultimate goal of reaching the top. That level is what we know as Heaven. I never saw the level called Heaven but I know it was there. I could hear angelic choirs singing and I felt nothing but pure love. That's where God resides and where we ultimately should want to go. I asked Rachel to describe the uppermost level to me. "The realm you know as Heaven, is the most magnificent place you could ever be. Think of the most peaceful and loving environment you've ever been in, a place void of fear, worries, judgement, and the troubles of life. It's where the rivers flow with nothing but everything that is right and good. Somewhere you can always feel safe in the arms of the one who created you. This is Heaven and it is perfect, because this is where you ultimately know God."

Let's take a life like Ghandi for example, one in which you have learned many great lessons. Your days are filled with prayer, meditation, thanksgiving, etc., you have no desire whatsoever for worldly possessions. When your time comes, you will cross to one of the upper levels.

This led me to think about where I would go when it's my time. I live a pretty good life. I try to practice the Golden Rule daily. I certainly don't do everything right necessarily but I try to help others, and at least I don't make a habit of hurting intentionally. I'm not saying I've never done anything wrong or hurt someone. But after my visit, I do stop now and think about life and my actions toward others. I know I won't cross to one of the highest levels but hopefully, I'll cross to somewhere in between, maybe similar to where I am now. Someone asked me if I know how many levels there really are. I have no idea and I don't know if we are meant for that information until we go home.

There's so much more to the story though, much more than my brain can comprehend. It's like I got the feeling that where we go is really not a literal place. I'm not saying it can't be though. The feeling bestowed on me was when we are not as spiritually advanced, we require more physical and material surroundings; my guess is because we still love those things. Personally, at this point in my life, I can't imagine crossing over and not having some of the things I enjoy here in this lifetime. That's because I'm still in the baby stages of my spiritual walk. Like I said, I'm definitely not on the lower rungs of the ladder but I still have a long way to go.

As we advance up the spiritual ladder, we no longer require those surroundings because we shed the material things of life. Let's focus on someone like Mother Teresa. We all know what a great woman she was. She devoted her adult life to God and helping others. I read an article once that gave her daily schedule and I was fascinated. Typically, she would be up and making herself ready for mass at 6am. After mass, she greeted people who came to see her and gave them blessings. From 7am – 1pm, she worked tirelessly talking with people who had problems, giving them encouragement and blessings. She helped anyone who might have been in need of her. Mother Teresa then spent her afternoon in prayer and thanksgiving with her sisters, as the Missionaries of Charity. This time was usually from 1pm – 4pm, and it was a time of prayer and inner reflection. Then after praying once again, she would spend late afternoon and evening being of service to others. The article I read spoke of how she was such a warm and caring individual who respected everyone.

Now in reading that description of Mother Teresa and her daily routine, one thing really stood out with me. The article stated that she was always smiling and filled with joy. Her heart seemed to constantly overflow just talking with people, praying, and bestowing blessings. No mention was ever made of her enjoying the luxuries of life that most of us do. I'm sure there were times she indulged in something she liked, but she found happiness and peace, in her walk with God and service to others. I have no doubt what so ever, when it came her time to cross over, I'm sure she saw what we know as the streets of gold. I believe she is right up there close to God. She shed the material and physical possessions, the earthly treasures, and traded them for a more spiritual walk.

I can tell you one thing, I know I have a ways to go because number one, I can't imagine not having my coffee in the morning. I joke with God all the time about how I admire those souls who can live on prayer. I'm a praying woman, always have been. In reading this book you know from past chapters how I believe in the power of prayer. But I'm telling you now, I've already told God when it really is my time, I'm bringing my Keurig with me and a basket full of coffee pods. I can't even begin to imagine being without apple pie and ice cream either. Yep, that's how I know what rung I'll be hanging onto on that spiritual ladder. You have to have a sense of humor, believe me the Other Side does.

I saw this sense of humor there. The Other Side is filled with laughter, well at least the upper levels are. God wants us to be happy, content, and feel loved. He wants us to know that we can have a sense of humor because they do. I witnessed the Angels entertaining each other, playing ball with children, playing catch with dogs. I witnessed the guides playing games of chess and a couple of board games involving playing pieces I didn't recognize. I think those were probably the middle level guides, ones that had to de stress from taking care of all of us on a daily basis. I'm sure it's not easy for them. I've said for a while that my guardian angel and guides have probably been at the point of a nervous breakdown many times.

At this stage, I knew something was about to happen. I felt I was going to have to make some type of decision. I was still asking questions and Rachel graciously answered; Lord, she must have had the patience of Job. There was so much I'd seen and learned but I craved to know all the answers. I wanted to stay there forever. I asked if children stayed children when they got back home or if they grow up. Rachel told me again that I was thinking in earthly terms. When babies and children cross back over, they always have family members there to care and nurture them until they are ready to learn more lessons. I saw the loving caregivers and guides, who had led countless lives in which they had learned many lessons of life. Rachel told me that before we ever incarnate, we decide ahead of time when we want to return home. "So our time is predetermined like I've been taught?" I asked. "In a matter of speaking," she said.

"Your teaching is definitely on the right track." Rachel said we choose when we want to come back based on lessons we schedule to be learned in a life. God and the Divine Council oversee each and every life in full support. I told her I always thought of God as regulating everything. She laughed and told me that God is all knowing and does oversee and know everything. From the very beginning of time, creation was much different then. It was simple, less complex, and in the very beginning there were no bad aspects of creation present. Then as time progressed, creation became very vast and complicated. God longed for those who would help to rule His creations.

Originally God intended for His divine creations and human creations to work in unison. He wanted each to help run the universe together. God's ultimate goal is for everyone to live in peace and harmony in the new Eden, which will be on Earth. I wasn't given the timeline on this, just the information. The Divine Council is God's right hand, but God always has the final say if there is any question.

Rachel said each time we incarnate, we choose three exit points. This means each one of us have three different times during a life we can choose to go back home. It was set up that way, so that we could learn what we needed to learn in stages while on earth. She said it wasn't that way in the very beginning because there was no need for it. But as time progressed, man became more materialistic; greed, malice, and evil became second nature to some. The time came when God stepped in and created the exit points. "So the exit points have not always existed?" I asked. "No, for example there was a time when man automatically lived to a great number of years. This was a more simple time, a time when disease and evil, as you know it, did not exist. Although it was not a perfect time, it was nothing like present time."

Rachel said as time progressed, so did all the bad aspects that could ever be thought of. God never intended for our world to be in this sad shape. She said it's been this way for thousands of years. Time came, when because of man's hatred toward one another, factors played in to the picture. Disease, famine, manmade disasters, ego, selfishness, pollution, weapons of war, political unrest, etc., became common; God had no choice but to step in and make a change.

Again, I was completely blown away by this. It was totally out of my safe zone, but after the things I'd seen, I knew I needed to be out of that safe feeling. I now craved learning everything I could about how the Universe really works. Rachel explained that life is tough; Earth is a school for learning. In truth, it would be very easy just to bail out every time we encountered hardships in life. If we did that, we would never learn anything at all. She explained that all souls are strong to a certain degree. But like people, some are not as strong as others. Don't you just love the way she explains things?

She gave me an example. On the one hand you have a soul that is a man. During his life here, he develops diabetes. The doctor tells him he must cut out sugar and change his diet. He must exercise and take good care of himself. This man chooses to follow that advice and lives to a ripe old age. Then we have the man who experiences the same situation only he chooses not to take care of himself. He eats all the wrong foods, does not exercise, and his body just deteriorates. It doesn't mean one way is more right or wrong, it's about choices. One man chooses to be stronger and take the bull by the horns, while the other man chooses not to.

Let's take the second example and break it down. Here we have the man that chose not to follow his doctor's advice. He lived life how he wanted and did so of his own free choice and free will. At the time, he and his wife had no children but were expecting a baby. A couple of weeks before the baby was born, he was hospitalized because of serious complications. He was told if his condition did not improve with antibiotics, he would stand a chance of losing his leg. The man was ready to give up. His body was tired and his soul desired to go back home and start again. His soul knew an exit point was coming up.

Then a miracle happened; his baby was born. Although he could not attend the birth, his wife was allowed to bring the baby to see him. When he saw that little baby, it was like his soul had something to live for all over again. He regained a purpose and chose to fight; he fought hard. Although he lost his leg, he did not lose his life. After that, he changed his ways and had a good life. Rachel said this is why the Creator made life this way. So souls who are not as strong, couldn't just choose to opt out. Each soul is given every chance possible to learn needed lessons. Because the man chose to stay and fight, he accomplished learning some of those.

Next was a man who had battled cancer. He fought bravely for several years but he was tired; his soul knew an exit point was getting close. Friends and family tried everything to help him get well. Even after receiving the best medical treatment, his soul still longed to return home. A few days before his return, he began having dreams, visions of those he'd left behind. He spoke of seeing his parents, who'd been gone for many years and his dear wife. Family and friends said he talked out of his head; that wasn't true. It was just the Other Side preparing him for the journey back home. When time came for the exit point, the door opened; his soul let go and the body died. He lived a commendable life but his body was old in earth years; he was tired. One could not blame him at all.

Another example was a woman who'd been in a horrible car accident. She had broken bones, internal bleeding, and burns over 20% of her body. She was in her mid –forties. Although her body was badly damaged, she still had exit points left. Her first exit point was when she was a child. She was bitten on the hand by a brown recluse spider, while playing around a wood pile. Although it was tough on her little body for a time, she chose not to take that exit point; she made a complete recovery. This time her soul decided to fight as well. Despite the accident, she wanted to get better. After many surgeries and hours of intensive therapy, she regained her strength. She eventually did quite well. Her soul knew it still had unfinished business. She wanted to finish that business so she opted to stay.

"So what happens when someone reaches that third exit point?" I asked. "As you might assume, when that time comes, it doesn't matter where you are or what you're doing; you're going home." "Do we all choose the same exit point years?" I asked. "Oh no, everyone is different. Most choose according to the experiences they've had in previous lives and according to lessons they still have to learn. You may have a soul that is going to reincarnate as a child with a serious birth defect. That soul knows in choosing that life it will cause much pain to the body and sadness for those that care for them. Because of this, that soul might choose their exit point in early years, say at the earthly ages of four, fifteen, and twenty-one years because of the severity. On the other hand you might have a soul that chooses to be born into a life of say your middle to upper class. That soul chooses to live a pretty good life, not really enduring any big hardships or health problems. That soul might choose exit points more spread out. Let's say maybe the first one at thirty-five years, then at sixty, and finally at ninety-five years of age."

But what about those souls who live to be older but their lives are filled with pain, hurt, and suffering like my Dad's life? "Those souls are some of the oldest of the old souls. They are the ones who have lived the most and learned the most lessons. They chose during their lives to endure many hardships, so as to learn and advance. Many times these dear souls are here in order for those around them to learn as well. They are known as Helper Souls. They are the ones who advance at a rapid pace because their ultimate goal is growing closer to the Creator. Many times they choose to advance by helping those who call upon them."

One more scenario was shown to me as well. This involved a precious little baby. Unfortunately, the mother and father regularly used drugs. They had done so for such a long time, it was just second nature to them. When the baby was born, it had multiple problems. The little fellow stayed in the NICU unit for weeks but his little body grew tired with each day. His parents were so upset by the way their child looked. They cried many tears and prayed that God would spare their baby. They buried him a week later with help from friends and family who donated money to do so. Because of this child, and the condition he was born with, the mother served time for a while. During her days in prison, she came to know God in a way she had never known before; she searched deep within. She wasn't brought up to know God, but this knowing and wanting to know just happened.

By this time her husband, who visited every few days, began to realize the change in her; he began to change as well. He no longer spent time around those doing drugs because every time he did, his mind flashed back to that baby. They talked about things they had never discussed before and how they could have done things differently. When the mother was released from prison, she and her husband made the decision to go through training to become counselors. They eventually worked with young people who had drug problems and helped to save many lives. Rachel showed me that although they never forgot their baby and the experience they had, many lives were helped because of them. I saw where that child came into this life for the soul purpose of helping his parents to overcome habits they never could break before. That baby helped them to learn much needed lessons.

There was so much for me to think about; I still felt I had a gazillion things to learn. Rachel took my hand. She told me because I'd crossed over between exit points, it would be my decision to stay or go back. She explained that sometimes we do things to our bodies to cause us undue stress and hardships. Sometimes this happens to the point where the body tries to exit before an exit point. It just gives out, and if it's not one of our exit points, then it is premature. What she said really made me stop and think about how I'd lived my life up until that point.

My childhood was stressful; the worry had followed me into my teen years and adulthood. At that point in my life, I was a chronic worrier; I stressed about everything. Rachel explained to me that when we worry about things instead of giving our worries over to God, we actually attract things we don't want. This was my first lesson about the Universal Law of Attraction. The Law of Attraction is defined as this, "You attract into your life those things, circumstances, and conditions that correspond with the nature of your dominant, habitual thoughts, and beliefs, both conscious and unconscious." Wow what a wakeup call for me. I knew at that point I had to learn how to give everything over and stop the chronic worrying cycle. I've known people, and I'm sure you have as well, who've made themselves sick worrying over a situation.

I asked if my family would be okay if I chose to stay. Rachel smiled and said, "Of course they will. I'm not saying they won't miss you but they will eventually be okay." Then I thought about my parents. They were on up in years and being an only child, I considered how they might need me. Rachel showed me a screen of possible life events in years to come if I chose to go back. She made it clear that these were possibilities based on free choice and free will. She explained that God and His team of helpers urge us, or give us the knowing for living life. Ultimately the life we choose to live is up to us. Again, that's the law of Free Choice and Free Will.

"If I did decide to return would it make a difference?" I asked. Rachel smiled at me and said, "Oh sweetie, you have no idea the difference you could make." She told me I would only be asked to do one thing. I should tell people, anyone who would listen, what Home or the Other Side is really like. She asked me to tell others about the joy, love, and peace anyone can have, if they choose too. She said the Creator wants all his children to know they are so loved. So many people are afraid when they die, there is no more. They feel they only get one chance and that's not the way it is. She told me if I decided to go back, that I would have teachers always around to help me. I asked how I would find these teachers and she said not to worry, they would find me. I found that to be very true, for they have on many occasions. This is where my present guide fits in. My family and many of my friends, have found great comfort in Red Cloud's words of wisdom through the years. Red

Cloud has been a source of goodwill and wisdom to many who have allowed him to be a part of their lives.

It was then I learned about the gifts that God bestows on every one of us before we are ever born. Rachel said these gifts are God's way of helping us out during a life. When a little child is born it is so innocent, sweet, and trusting. That child has faith that she will be taken care of. Then life happens and that little child begins to grow up. She begins to lose her memories of home; those memories begin to fade. It is within the time of that fading, her natural gifts become suppressed. Sometimes a child is born into a culture where these gifts and talents are nurtured. The child may grow to be a great spiritual teacher with great insight. Still others are born into a culture where this kind of thing is not talked about. Because of this the child grows into an adult that has no idea whatsoever, that she even has gifts given by God.

Rachel said people who go through near death experiences are given the chance to reclaim and remember those gifts and talents. She said God's word tells us, they are to be used. They are to shine and be used for good and the good of helping others. I told her I had made the decision to go back because I wanted to live the remainder of my life in service to others. I wanted people to know what I was blessed enough to learn through my experience. There is so much more I would love to share with you. I wish this book could go on forever. As I walked away from Rachel, she motioned for me to look at a movie screen. She played for me a quick clip as a parting gift.

In that movie, I saw many other worlds that God created; a few like ours and others very different. There were endless planets, not just the ones we know and are taught about. I saw those who live on other planets; some look similar to us, some very different. Others were different colors and some I would have a hard time describing; it was amazing. I saw not only the great flood of Noah's day but many great floods that our earth had encountered since creation. I saw our earth and her past civilizations, much of them being as advanced, or more advanced than ours. I learned that everything, including the earth, runs in cycles. I saw where beings travel between planets in crafts not of this world and how some of these beings are here on earth. They're here to help us; still others are here for their own gain. I saw the beautiful and majestic wonders of some of the other planets, the lush vegetation, and amazing colors. It was comforting how their inhabitants worked together for the good of their planets.

Then I witnessed the great awakening of earth. I saw how there will be more and greater natural disasters, some being at the hand of man. There will be great hardships that will arise on our planet, extensive flooding, earthquakes, and vast food shortages; many people perished. Rachel touched my shoulder. "These things must take place for the earth and her people, so she may reclaim who she once was. Man must reclaim his spiritual roots given in the beginning by God." Rachel showed me not only does man have to satisfy karmic debt but everything in existence has karmic debt. Mother earth has been in the stages of revolt and taking back what is hers for some time now. I saw how man has abused earth for so long, there is no choice but for these things to happen.

One of the most disturbing points I was shown, was results from the suppressed cure for cancer. Knowing there has been a cure for this dreaded and deadly disease for many years, there have been, and still are, those who willingly follow and support this suppression. I saw faces and bodies of those ravaged by this disease; I saw the hurt and loss of lives. I felt sick at how the greed of man has taken over. My eyes were opened to the enormous amount of money that has lined pockets of those powerful individuals, the luxuries they have acquired, and the lifestyles they live. All these earthly possessions gained, at the expense of innocent men, women, and children. How sad man let himself evolve to this point.

Another disturbing scene was that of how our children and animals are treated. This atrocity has gone on for some time, but the days we live in now, are plagued by evil. There are people who commit crimes against children and animals; when I saw these scenes, it left me physically sick. Rachel assured me that no one goes unpunished when they commit such crimes. She explained how Jesus loves and cares so for all the children and animals. "They are innocent in their own ways. They depend on those who will love and care for them. They depend on families and caregivers for survival. Those who commit crimes against these precious children and animals will receive such harsh punishment they will desire only to die." When I heard these words, I could sense the change in Rachel's voice. I knew she meant what she said. I believe in my heart there is a special place for those who commit such acts.

I saw hope, where there would once again be a peaceful time on Earth. Our planet is now in her final hours before the return of the Christ Consciousness. It makes me sad to think, so many bad things that are going to happen, could be avoided if only man would wake up and change his evil ways. There will be much civil unrest and violence; there will be weather calamities and food shortages. Some of these events have already begun but it will only get worse. I wonder how bad it will be by the time this book is released. Today is Sunday, July 10th, 2016. Civil unrest is rising up everywhere. Many states are feeling it, as well as my home state of SC. Only the Good Lord above knows what's going to happen around election time. The Other Side has no way of knowing a timeline for these events. It's up to man and his free choice and free will. But, eventually a time of peace will emerge and man will awaken once again to his spiritual side. I know there was so much more but I can't remember everything. As hard as I try, it was just not meant for me to.

While staring at the movie screen, I felt myself getting very sleepy. When I opened my eyes, I was back at home. My husband was talking to me, asking what in the world was taking me so long. I stared at him to the point he asked if I was alright. "How long has it been since you went out to the car?" I asked. "About ten minutes, why?" he asked. All of that in a ten minute time span. Wow! Did that ever confirm time here and time back home is very different.

Not a day goes by I don't think of the happenings of that day. I still recall my experience and feel so very blessed I could be a part of understanding how the Universe works for a short time. There have been many people who've experienced what I did. Again, you cannot possibly know the impact it has on you unless you experience it for yourself. I only hope through my words, you can somehow understand a little better how great our God is and how we are all so connected and loved. We're not alone; we're never alone in any situation. There are spiritual helpers everywhere, they love and care for all of us if we only allow them too.

Chapter Eight

I'm Always Amazed

Several years ago, while writing one morning at the kitchen table, my mind raced in a thousand different directions. I found myself once again having problems concentrating on one thing in particular. I think with most of us who've had NDE's, it seems to follow that pattern as we try to recreate our experience; there's just so much to process. It's as if you're a well bubbling up. When you try and write it down, it's like all the things you experienced, and still continue to experience, run together; they overlap, twist and turn, etc. You have no idea how often I've sat perplexed, staring at my computer. I've rewritten lines a hundred times because what the heart needs to say can be so hard to put into words.

While making his coffee my husband asked, "Why so gloomy?" I must have looked pretty deep in thought. Or maybe I had that first thing in the mid-morning Medusa hair; maybe the face buried in the hands with one eye peeking out, been up since 3am look. Who knows, but my body language and appearance must have screamed, "Help me." I told him I wasn't even sure at the time I should be writing this book. No one would probably believe me anyway. While sipping to make sure his creamer was just right, my husband chuckled and offered his sage advice. His kind words are always appreciated in these tense situations; it happens a lot.

Many times I've been discouraged to the point of locking all my writings away, safe and secure from eyes and ears that might not understand. My sweet hubby would always put things into perspective for me and that "aah" feeling would somehow make it all better. It might not always be what I wanted to hear but none the less, something I needed to hear. If not him, it's usually one of the kids or one of my friends putting their two cents worth in. Believe me, there are times I desperately need pep talks.

There were, and still are occasions, I've felt like pounding my head on the table because my brain feels like it wants to explode. I guess I always will be hesitant to share some of the things I know about how the Universe works. For many years, it wasn't easy talking about a near death experience; especially when you live in the Bible belt. You'd think it would be a great place to tell your story to those who will listen. Oh it can be, but in the beginning I had issues, real issues. I was afraid of being branded a heretic, a backslider, or even worse burnt at the stake. I've had less than cordial encounters many times in past years; thankfully I can handle them much better now.

One of those times in particular comes to mind when recalling a conversation I had with a lady that actually approached me. This is most often the case because I generally keep to myself. I don't go around subjecting people to my beliefs; when you're from a small town, word gets around. Wherever you go, about four out of every ten times someone will ask a question or two or share something that has happened to them. I don't mind this at all. I love and enjoy talking with people, sharing and helping when I can. But, every now and then you get someone who seems to be fishing for answers. They don't care what you tell them, they're not going to believe you anyway.

This woman, we'll call her Tonya, approached me about her husband having a heart attack while seeing another woman. She asked me a general question about him and my thoughts on the subject. Seems harmless enough doesn't it? That's what I used to think too, ha. I listened intently for about twenty minutes, even though I was really in a hurry; it was clear she was out for revenge. I seemed to make it worse by telling her that God loves everyone, even her husband and how I was sure he was met by loving family members when he crossed over. I'm here to tell you that statement sent her into a tizzy. "For Heaven sakes, that doesn't sound anything like what I was taught in church. I know he's in the pits of Hell for what he did." After that, she pretty much blessed me out.

You would've thought I'd just committed an immortal sin by making that statement. I tell you this little story, and I have dozens of these same scenarios, so that maybe you'll find yourself more able to understand what I went through in the beginning; it's a lot different now. Every now and then I still come across someone that makes me feel like running into a closet and locking the door.

*   *   *

It was a beautiful morning, just gorgeous outside. My house was clean, clothes were washed, groceries bought, and supper in the crock pot. I'd said the day before I felt some writing time coming on. As crazy as it sounds, in order for me to have a productive writing day, the conditions have to be right. By right, I mean my chores have to be done and everything in order. Yes, I'm fully aware of how OCD I am. That was actually discussed in depth when I crossed to the other side. I'm much better than I used to be, thank you very much.

Just the day before, a lady I know approached me in the store. We talked about this and that and as usual my spiritual side came out because of something she said. After about ten minutes on a certain subject, she blasted me right in the middle of the Ingles Supermarket. Yep, right there in the fruit and produce; all because I made a statement she didn't agree with. She put her finger in my face and told me that I didn't know what I was talking about. She said I just needed to keep my opinions, ideas, or whatever you call it to myself; she walked off and that was that. I stood there for a minute reflecting on how she'd approached me, not vice versa.

I know you find it hard to believe that could happen to me but it did and it does. I walked out to my car that day, put my groceries in, returned my buggy, sat down, and ask myself, "Wow! What just happened in there?" She was so loud and obnoxious with her comments, the produce man walked over after she'd left and asked if I was okay. I smiled and told him I guessed it was just one of those days.

Experiences of that severity leave me mentally drained. It was a similar situation I had, that taught me there are some people who are classified as "Energy Vampires." Believe it or not, for those of you who've never heard the term it's real, very real. These people will drain every ounce of life out of you if you don't get away from them. The term energy vampire, is defined as people who are emotionally immature individuals who have the sense that the whole world revolves around them. Their perspective on life and the way they were raised to believe is all that matters. They're almost incapable of seeing things from another person's views. In layman's terms, it's going to be their way or no way.

I can think of several people that fit this description and I don't associate with them unless I have too. When I do, I make it short and sweet. I honestly think if you take a moment and think about it, you may know of one or two of them yourself; they are everywhere. It seems that every time you're around them, they talk non- stop. You can hardly get a word in edge wise; you're doing most of the listening. After they've gone over every subject they feel is important, they start over. They indicate to you they want to know your opinion and how you feel but in reality, it's a trap. They don't want your opinion on anything; they just want to use you as a sounding board to vent. Lord, if I were a therapist I'd be rich.

Many times I've found these people constantly live in the past. They can't get around certain issues they have with certain people, therefore they are just stuck. Because they're stuck, they want you to be stuck with them. They talk about the same things over and over. Does this give new meaning to the term "broken record?" Heaven forbid you get up the courage to voice your opinion or make a comment that doesn't agree with their belief system. I'm tired just thinking about it.

I've come to a conclusion these past few years, that no subject will stir your dander up or ruffle your feathers more than religion. Lord, I can't even begin to tell you the conversations I've had with people about their religious views. I had a lady tell me one day that she knew beyond the shadow of a doubt, the man accused of breaking in her church was guilty. When I ask her why, she said it was because he sneezed when the sheriff asked if he'd committed the crime. Like an idiot, I asked how she came about knowing this. She replied that her preacher preached about it when she was growing up. I'm telling you now I was speechless; I'm still running from that one.

Many times I worked myself into a frenzy trying to say the right words. I found once I really studied on it, I was being held back from my true message out of fear. Fear that something I said, would offend someone and their beliefs. I can tell you this for sure; the Other Side tells me that our world is made up of many different beliefs. It only stands to reason that wherever and however we are raised, that is the belief system most of us follow unless we get out of dodge. The Other Side says that as long as our beliefs lead us to do good and not hurt one another, it's right, no matter how they differ.

*   *   *

One week in particular I'd been praying and talking to God and Mama a lot. I explained how I was at a standstill with my writing and needed help. I struggled so it made my head hurt just trying to put words on paper. For many years, I knew what the words were and what I needed to say but I refused to listen to my gut instinct in doing that. Why do you think it's taken so long to complete this book? I worried so much about not offending certain people with my writings, that it caused some major blockages. This is what happens when we don't use our talents that God gives us, like they're supposed to be used. How many times in your life have you struggled with what you need to do and what you really do, for fear of offending someone? Many of you, like me, have at some point said those immortal words, "If only I'd done what I needed to do instead of listening to everyone else, I'd be okay."

I've since learned to listen to that deep sense of knowing. I find I'm all the better for it. I pray and ask God to just throw me out a sign when I need it. I've always done that and to this day, it works great for me. It was one of those, "throw that sign right out and hit me in the face with it," moments when my body began to tingle a little. Through the years I've come to realize when this happens, something significant or amazing is about to take place.

I've always been very intuitive but after my NDE, that gift just seemed to magnify. Many times I walk into a store or happen upon someone that makes me tingle, and it's not the way you think either. It can be a good thing or a not so good thing, that goes for world happenings as well. Many times, I just know something is about to take place because my body heats up in a certain way and I feel kind of bubbly. There was a time I was convinced it was hot flashes, ha ha. This has happened to us several times when leaving out on a run and it always ends up with mechanical failure with the truck, or something of that nature. That gut feeling of mine once again surfaced on a particular morning and what happened next left me speechless.

Guerry was making his coffee, while attempting to carry on a conversation with me. I have a habit of saying things like, "Oh Yeah," or "I know what you mean," when I'm in deep thought about something and staring at my computer screen. He says that's usually a signal to him I'm not really paying much attention at all; my youngest son has cautioned me about this a lot. I tend to remind them how we wives and mothers are wonderful at multi-tasking. So for the sake of giving them credit, it was one of my half way paying attention modes where I caught a glimpse of something from the corner of my eye. I saw Guerry make kind of a funny face, as I focused on what we were seeing. Honestly, he saw it before I did. I guess that's what happens when you live with someone who converses with the Other Side; yep, it eventually rubs off on you.

I think we both zeroed in on the same spot within seconds of each other. We were definitely trying to decide what the other was seeing. It was like a little pocket just opened up in mid- air and out of that pocket a shiny penny fell out. It spun around on the table a few times, stopped, and fell over. We both stared at each other, then at the penny, then at each other again. I had no idea what just took place but for a couple of minutes, I was totally at a complete loss for words. Are you having those, "she's totally nuts," thoughts yet? "That looks like a brand new penny," Guerry said. He picked it up, the date on it was from 1963, the year I was born.

I had no doubt at that very moment, it was from Mama because she'd told me in later years that even though she had a rough time after I came along, 1963 was the best year of her life. It was the year of new beginnings. The year God saw fit to give her a little baby girl to raise. She said she would always be thankful and grateful. I still have that penny tucked away in a safe place so as never to spend it; many times I've felt it has brought me comfort and good luck.

*   *   *

The year after mama passed away, I'd had her on my mind a lot. It was my birthday and we were working in the yard. Fall is my favorite time of the year. Seeing that my birthday is October 1st, it always gets me in the mood for scarecrows and mums. Everything and anything to do with pumpkins screams me. I was raking around one of the big oak trees when all of a sudden, I caught a glimpse of something; it almost took my breath away. Attached to the side of that 50 year old oak was the fattest and most colorful caterpillar I'd ever seen. He was so fluffy and fat, he didn't even look real; it was nothing like I'd ever seen before. He was about 8 inches long. His body was as fat around as golf balls and divided into four sections.

He had the little black feelers and eyes that made him look almost comical. His first section was lime green, then red, orange, with the last section being yellow. He just looked at me like he was my friend and had known me forever; I yelled for Guerry to see him. "Wow, I've never seen anything that looks like that, it's amazing." Daddy was on the deck supervising with his eyes all bugged out; he said he'd never seen a caterpillar like that anywhere. What made it even more amazing was it triggered a memory of my Mama; I've learned that's how they work. Those that have already gone on, do things to trigger our memories to let us know they're still here.

When I was just a little girl my Mama loved to write. She had a talent for it. She had notebook pages full of stories and such. One year for my birthday, she wrote me a story called "The Fuzzy Wuzzy Caterpillar." She drew pictures of him on the pages and I loved for her to read it to me; it was my favorite. I actually learned in later years there were other poems and stories by that name. But, that was okay because the one Mama wrote for me, was my very own. The caterpillar on the tree looked just like the one from her story. I smiled because I knew it was her way of saying "Happy Birthday." We left him alone to do his own thing but I was all smiles that day because it was very special to me.

Now, you might say, "Oh that's only a coincidence" like a lot of things that happen seem to be. But if something brings you even one moment of joy and happiness, then who are we to question. I've learned when something happens and a departed loved one comes to mind, it's just their way of saying, "Hey, I'm still here with you, I never left." Again, these stories I tell you are of things I've personally witnessed, in hopes you can know how close your loved ones are to you as well.

*   *   *

Daddy had a Farmall Cub tractor when I was young; he used it for plowing up the garden and cutting grass. It had a big mowing deck on it and I delighted in the fact that daddy had taught me how to mow. I always looked forward to climbing up in the seat of that red tractor. Daddy had just put a shiny new muffler on top of it and away I went. Little did I know that in just a few minutes, my whole world would briefly turn upside down.

That's what happens as a child when you don't pay attention to where you're going because you're too busy watching a cat fight with a snake. A few seconds later, I ran up under a low hanging limb from the pear tree and bent the brand new muffler almost all the way over. I was terrified because I'd done that. All I could think about was straightening that shiny new muffler back up. When I grabbed it, my whole hand stuck to the scorching hot metal; when I pulled my hand loose, my skin went with it.

I stared at the skin from my hand still stuck to the muffler. Daddy heard me stop the tractor and scream. He came running, only to find me trying to climb down with my hand looking like something out of a sci fi movie. The look on his face was enough; I knew it was bad and it hurt like heck. Daddy put me in the truck and off to Dr. Smith's office we went. He took one look at it, cleaned it up, and told daddy it was third degree burns. He said normally he would send me to the hospital but we all knew Ma Bracken could talk the fire out. He suggested we go there; he would call ahead.

We pulled in front of their house; Mr. and Mrs. Bracken were sitting on the porch. They were fine people, the finest you would ever meet and loved by all. Mrs. Bracken helped me to the kitchen and pulled out a chair. It was a horrible burn, so bad it made me sick at my stomach to look at it. Daddy and Mr. Bracken stayed out on the porch. My hand hurt so bad it was shaking. All I could think of was how stupid it was to touch that hot muffler.

She told me to close my eyes. She took my hand in hers and assured me everything would be fine because God would see to it. She told me to think of something beautiful, maybe a beautiful place I loved to go and concentrate on that. I could hear her talking in a very low voice. She was talking to God no doubt, reciting something from the Bible. I was hurting too bad to remember what it was but I knew it was biblical. When I had my near death experience, I was blessed enough to get answers to many of my questions; finding out how Ma Bracken talked the fire out was one of them.

Certain people have this gift; it's the gift of touch healing. It's been practiced since the beginning of time. Here in the South, people just automatically know about these things. We have folks who not only talk fire out but those who stop blood, cure thrush, talk poison oak off, and warts. I've personally witnessed three of these happenings take place on several different occasions. Problem is that times are changing; we no longer say stopping the blood, etc. The ones who do practice these sacred acts term themselves many times now as "Energy Healers." Well I can tell you first and foremost that people tend to run from that because they have no idea it's all connected.

Put a hundred folks from my area in a room. Tell them that you have fine Christian people available to stop blood, talk warts off, talk poison oak off, cure your babies thrush, etc.; they'll not only line up but they'll put in some serious money when the plate is passed around. Now on the flip side, you put that same hundred folks in a room. Tell them you have energy healers available to help with any needs they may have such as warts, poison oak, headaches, backaches, chakra clearing, etc., and ninety five of them will make a new back door getting out of there. Next thing you know, they'll be in the parking lot accusing those energy healers of doing the devil's work. Please folks, break out of the glass houses you live in and realize that God still has people here that can do these things.

These particular scenarios always come to mind when someone talks about communing with demons and how the Bible is against those practices. It still amazes me to this day how some people can accuse you of beings in cahoots with evil spirits, yet they think its fine to talk the fire out, speak in tongues, stop blood, etc. It all comes from the same source folks and that source is the Other Side. But, like everything else, you must learn to communicate with the good and not the bad side of anything.

As I sat there in Mrs. Bracken's kitchen, my mind drifted to scenes of fishing with daddy on the creek bank. The water was cold and clear as it flowed over the rocks. I thought of how peaceful it was. All of a sudden, I felt a tingle go through my entire body, sort of like it was heating up and tingling at the same time. Then my feet felt like they were tingling. It was like a rush of electricity moved through my whole body and out that hand. I felt immediate relief; the burning stopped. Ma Bracken patted me on the head and told me to open my eyes. She gave me some salve and said to keep it on my hand for three days until it was better; at the end of the third day, it would be alright.

After the third day we took the bandage off, my hand was completely headed. There was no visible scarring at all, just a little pink; it was like it had never happened. That same day we stopped by Dr. Smith's office so he could see. He just looked at Daddy, shook his head, and said, "Well, that's definitely a miracle because that was third degree burns." He said he knew that God and Ma Bracken were better than any hospital.

*   *   *

My Daddy loved all of his Great Grand Children; he and Mama were the best. Daddy was blessed enough to be in my Grandson's lives for several years but he only knew my Granddaughter Khloe for a short time. My son and his family lived with us when Khloe was born. From the very beginning, Daddy bonded with her. By this time, he'd had his stroke but only recovered about seventy-five percent. Although he couldn't pick her up, he would sit and hold her; you could just see the love in his eyes. He would talk, make funny noises, and faces. As she grew older, he delighted in seeing her every day and my Daughter in Law Kayla was so good with him. She and Khloe brought a lot of comfort while others were working. He just lit up when Khloe came into the room. I can still see his sweet smile and hear, "there's Papa's doll." He couldn't do a lot by this time but he could play peep eye with her and blow kisses. I can't count the times I saw him doing this; it was so sweet. Khloe was less than two years old when Daddy passed.

One day Khloe and I were in the grocery store. She was sitting in the buggy as we strolled down the aisles. If you go to our local BiLo, the ladies always give the kids a cookie from the bakery dept. Khloe was all smiles as she enjoyed her cookie. All of a sudden, she leaned to my side and looked back like she was staring at someone. She got the biggest smile ever on her little face and started waving. I didn't pay it much attention at first but after several minutes of her doing this, I turned around to see who she was waving at. No one was there, so I just kind of shrugged and went on. Then she did the same thing again, only this time she giggled. She handed me the remnant of her cookie and put her hands over her eyes. I stood there and watched as she began to play peep eye; she did this several times.

Once again, I turned around only to find one lady all engrossed in her coupons searching through the coffee. Khloe once again stared into thin air. She laughed and said, "peep eye." By this time, I had no idea who she was playing with. "Are you playing peep eye with somebody Khloe?" I asked. Without even looking at me she pointed, shook her head yes, and said, "Papa." I turned around again then looked back at her. "You're playing peep eye with Papa?" She shook her head yes and did this the entire time we were in the store. We checked out and as we were walking out of the store, she began waving and saying bye; then she began blowing kisses. I almost froze in my tracks because that's what the two of them always did. I asked who she was blowing kisses at; she pointed and said, "there's Papa."

Now say what you want to folks, but children that age don't know how to lie. They call it like they see it and I have no doubt whatsoever, Khloe saw Daddy that day, she saw her Papa. How many of you have had children tell you they see someone that you can't? Or maybe you've heard of a child doing this. It's happened and still happens many times because children are so innocent. They have no judgement or inhibitions; they can simply see what we don't allow ourselves to lots of times.

*   *   *

After Christmas one year we headed to the beach for a few days with our good friends Roman and Sue. We decided to go out to eat one evening after a day of shopping because we were all starving. Now in case you don't already know it, water is a great conduit for the spirit world; so being at the beach makes it even better. When you pair that up with the fact that it was raining cats and dogs that evening, the conditions were just right for all kinds of messages to be coming through. Sometimes it's just not the time or place for a message though, especially if you're hungry and tired. But, when you have a very persistent spirit, one that is actually standing by a table of four people, you know something is up.

I'd already tried to head off the antics of this particular resident of the Other Side, "No way, absolutely not; I'm not going to do this right now," was the message I relayed. It did no good at all. She continued to stare at me the entire time we were eating; it was clear she had very important business for someone at that table. It's one of those times you feel torn as to what to do. I decided upon leaving I'd go with my gut and see what she had to say; Sue said she'd go with me. As we approached their table, my stomach did a little topsy- turvy thing and my body began to tingle. I was trying to decide how on earth I would approach them on the way over.

Sue and I stepped up to the table and gave them a big ole smile. "Hey folks," I said, "how are you enjoying your meal?" At this point I just hoped they didn't think I was a manager and start complaining about something. They were very cordial and said hello back. This was one of those times when you're really not sure what you're going to say; you just kind of go with the flow and hope you don't drown in the process. "Well folks, I'm not really sure how to say this but I can talk with those dearly departed souls who have already crossed over." This is usually the point I stop for a minute and study their expressions. When they didn't ask me to leave, I decided to press on.

I have a spirit here who identifies herself as Gladys. She's being very persistent and that leads me to believe at least one of you may know her. Does the name Gladys ring a bell with anyone? By this time, the two older gentlemen and the one older lady were all staring at me; there goes hearing that pin drop again. The other lady was clearly focused on her meal; I felt bad at this point for interrupting. That same lady put her fork down and looked up at me. "Gladys was my mother," she said in a monotone voice. I looked over at Gladys; I felt that she was bearing such a burden, like a feeling of guilt. I could honestly feel she'd bore this weight since her passing.

"Mam, your mother is telling me how sorry she is that she never showed affection when you were growing up. She said she was a very stubborn woman." "You got that right," the lady said, "she was stubborn as the day is long." I could definitely sense the table getting a little tense. "She's telling me if she could live this life over again, that she would have done things so much different. She says she's so sorry she never supported you and encouraged you to follow your dreams. She wants you to know that she loves you very much and hopes you can forgive her for being that way."

I knew at this point I'd done all I could do. It was the "don't shoot the messenger feeling." It was now up to the daughter. She stared at me and said, "Young lady let me tell you something. I was never close to my mother and I've been praying about this very situation for a while. I asked for God to send me some kind of sign and I thank you for this. I always loved her and I do forgive her." I felt an instant rush of peace all over my body and once again, I knew in some small way I'd been able to help someone. I thanked them for letting me intrude; they told me I needed my own television show.

Chapter Nine

Mama Knew

I knew my mama loved me growing up, we just weren't close. It wasn't until my children were almost grown, that we actually developed a Mother Daughter bond. By this time, Mama was in her seventies. Many days I still reflect on those years; Mama was a lot like me. She stayed busy and always had a project going. She loved to be productive. I guess it came from all the years she worked so hard when Daddy was sick. If I had to choose her mantra it would be words taken from Franklin D. Roosevelt, "Happiness is not in the mere possession of money; it lies in the joy of achievement, in the thrill of creative effort."

By the time she retired and gave up catering, her health had rapidly gone down; she was limited as to what she could do. Even though I'm far from retiring, I'm to the point in life where I can slow down some now. I can enjoy a little traveling and playing with the Grandchildren more. Many times I look at them and think how happy I would be if Mama were here to enjoy them with me. It was a sad day when she passed away; it was sudden. I would never have dreamed in a million years she would've had a massive heart attack. The kids and I are always talking about something she said or did and those memories bring floods of tears to my eyes often.

From as far back as I can remember my Mama was terrified of dying. I never understood where her fear came from. It was so real that when a preacher talked about the rapture and the second coming, Mama would sometimes get physically sick at her stomach. In our area, it's common to hear that a lot. Matter of fact some older folks say if a Man of God don't preach hellfire and brimstone, then he's not really preaching. I recall a couple of preachers myself growing up that frequented the pulpit in that manner. Many times I've sat through a revival scared to death and shaking.

Mama didn't talk about it much but she also had a fear of being buried alive. After my near death experience, I understood in great detail why she had those fears. There are more people than you know who wrestle with that same demon; that's another story for another book. I can remember Mama telling Daddy many times that he better make sure she was cremated. Daddy would get that frown on his face and tell her absolutely not; she would say ashes to ashes and dust to dust. Daddy didn't believe in cremation, simply because our family never observed that particular rite of passage; anyone who passed away was always buried. You see once again how you can fall into a pattern. Just because your family has always done something a certain way, doesn't always mean it's right for you. Her argument to daddy was that many people had been buried alive and she didn't want to be one of them.

Daddy talked about God, Heaven, Hell, and everything in between he'd been brought up with without a second thought. Mama was faithful to attend church, even though she didn't always agree with certain teachings; rather than disagree with Daddy, she just didn't talk about it. One belief she really had faith in, was the power of prayer; she'd witnessed the power it held many times. To this day I still miss her praying for me, especially when I asked for prayers for a specific reason. I could always count on her to pray her heart out. She also believed in the supernatural; she told me she'd had many experiences involving the unexplained. She definitely believed in the laying on of hands, talking the fire out, stopping blood, etc.

Mama worked and retired from Milliken & Company after forty plus years of faithful service. She loved her job as plant secretary and she was very good at it. Many times I recall her coming home after work to immediately start on a project; the woman literally never rested. When Mama retired, her intention was to help me in my baking business. At the time we owned a restaurant and had a small bakery in town. It was actually a dream Mama and I'd both always had. She loved coming up there baking and decorating cakes, making cookies, talking to people, etc. After all, she'd done that for forty years.

One morning Daddy called me to say that she couldn't get out of bed. I remember saying, "well she must be pretty tired then, just let her rest." To which he replied, "no, she cannot get out of the bed." I rushed down the road to their house; I found her lying there unable to barely move. Her arms would work. She could turn her head but her breathing wasn't right. She could feel her legs but they were swollen and very sore; she said they wouldn't cooperate. We immediately thought she'd had a stroke because some signs seemed to point that way. I suggested we call an ambulance but she wouldn't hear of it. We helped her to sit up and swing her legs off the side of the bed; with help she could stand, it just took forever. I do remember thinking what a good sign that was. After she limbered up a bit, she could actually slide her feet with one of us on each side holding her. I could tell she was in a great deal of pain; with each movement she would close her eyes and gasp. It was a long way through the house to go outside but we finally managed to get her into my car. She insisted on seeing Dr. Smith, our town's country doctor.

We'd called ahead; Dr. Smith was waiting at the back door. He came out and immediately cut up with her to lighten the mood. I can remember him saying, "now Betty, I've been telling you to quit running those marathons." After several questions, taking her blood pressure, temperature, etc., he stood back, scratched his head, and said something definitely wasn't right. He said he had an idea what it might be but only test would confirm it. He told us to take her straight on to the ER. Two days, and a battery of tests later, they determined she had a very aggressive form of Lupus. Lupus is defined as a chronic inflammatory disease that occurs when your body's immune system attacks its own tissue and organs. Inflammation caused by Lupus can affect many different body systems including your joints, skin, kidneys, blood cells, brain, heart, and lungs. Eventually, most of that happened to her.

Mama had always had problems with bronchitis, pneumonia, etc. One doctor had told her many years earlier she had weak lungs. We knew she had polio when she was young and the doctor seemed to think some of her issues stemmed from that. He told us that problems from polio, if severe enough, could show up many years later in different forms. He seemed to believe it was a combination of both. After her diagnosis, she was told by her rheumatologist she'd had lupus in her body for twenty-five years or more. He said when it decided to finally rear its ugly head and come out, it showed up full force.

Mama was never the same after that day. I watched that strong woman, the strongest woman I'd ever known, decline over the next few years. She was always such a go getter; she was involved in so many things. But in the years following her diagnosis, her body dwindled until it finally claimed her life in 2009. Her mind was still sharp as a tack the day she died; her poor body was just worn out. During that time she suffered as much as daddy, if not more. The other side cautions me all the time about the importance of rest and sleep, which is something Mama did not do well. I'm told we have to have a certain amount of rest for our bodies to fight off disease; makes sense doesn't it?

The first time medicine was prescribed for her was quite an experience. Mama retired at 62 to be with daddy after his retirement. Their plan was to buy a camper and do a little traveling. Daddy frowned on the idea because of being an MP in the army. He traveled often and his way of thinking was he'd done that enough in his lifetime. She convinced him that traveling would be fun for them because she was always working and never got the chance. About the time he came to terms with the idea, boom, it hit her only a few months later.

Because she retired early she wasn't eligible for Medicare. She still had about two and a half years before taking advantage of that. There was my mama who'd gone her whole adult life taking care of daddy who was now doing fine. The woman who was never sick except for some respiratory infections and a cough that lasted on and off for years. Mama was all set to do the Cobra insurance thing at retirement for the time allowed but Daddy said, "There's no need, you'll be fine. If you need medicine we'll just pay out of pocket because it won't be that much." Mama scoffed at the idea because her way of thinking was always to be cautious and prepared. Daddy won the argument and it would be a win that would cost them dearly.

They were like many folks in our area that worked in the textile industry; they worked hard and paid everything off. When they retired they had accumulated their savings, retirement, etc. They were only going to spend a little of it. I mean everything they owned was paid for. The rest would be left alone in case of an emergency. They figured it would last them, along with their social security, until they passed away. Mama always planned for a rainy day as she would say. From where they were standing and looking in, they were pretty set and they'd worked hard all those years to get to that point.

Mama's first visit to the Rheumatologist was a real eye opener. I drove them there; by this time she could at least get in and out of the car much easier. She'd been given some type of anti-inflammatory drugs. It took a few weeks to get in her system and she seemed to be feeling better. The doctor from the hospital told her that she would need to fall under the care of a specialist. After reviewing all the test results, he developed his plan of action. He'd hoped the disease would go into remission, it did for several years. But the day showed up when it became even more aggressive, causing severe crippling Rheumatoid Arthritis, which was very painful.

After the first visit, we took her home, she was worn out. Daddy went to the drug store to fill her medicine; he was gone what seemed like forever. I met him outside and asked how it went. He looked as pale as a ghost. He told me he waited on the prescriptions. The pharmacist had called him up to the counter. He asked if he'd been told that the medicine was very expensive; he said no one had mentioned it. The total for one month would be $3700.00. One of the drugs alone was $1700.00 and she'd been prescribed nine; I almost fell over. My heart sank; I honestly couldn't believe what I was hearing. "Are you kidding me?" I asked. "Your Mama is going to have a fit," he said, "she wanted to take better insurance from work; I told her she didn't need it."

He was exactly right, she most certainly did have a fit but she was a realist. Mama knew there was nothing she could do about it. She stayed on those nine medications for four months and she did make remarkable improvements. If I had to put a percentage on it, I'd say she improved about forty percent. We were very thankful for it. At the end of the four months, the doctor was able to take her off the two most expensive drugs. He substituted them with something more reasonable that would be less harsh on her body. Now keep in mind we had no idea just what these drugs, and the daily use of them, would eventually do to her. We were naïve about the effects that would lead to teeth loss, brittle bones, and eventually weakening of her heart.

The days passed by, some good and some bad. Sometimes she would be so tired she could hardly get out of bed. Can you even begin to imagine how hard that must have been for her? This was a woman who'd never known anything but hard work and staying busy. I was at her house one day; she had just finished cleaning the bathroom. She looked at me so pitiful and said, "You know, I've cleaned that bathroom hundreds of times from start to finish in less than 20 minutes or so. Today, it took me two hours." My heart sank the depths of the ocean when she told me that.

I saw the hurt and disgust of no longer being able to do the things she once did. Her body would no longer cooperate with her brain; she kept going and pushing for many years. Yes it slowed her down, but it didn't keep her down. The arthritis eventually damaged the cartilage in her feet to the extent she could never walk barefoot again, but she still kept going. I still remember how sore her feet became. We tried every type of insert we could find, even cutting pieces of thick foam to put in her shoes but nothing helped. She finally had to get special shoes made that were fitted and formed, they were super outrageous. Guerry still talks about the first time he met her many years ago, she was walking on crutches. She did this for quite a while. Her feet got so bad the crutches would help to steady her.

Even after many years of living with lupus, she still continued to cater a few weddings. My cousin Linda and I helped her as much as we could. The very last wedding mama catered she had gotten so bad that her hands no longer cooperated like she needed them too. I've seen that woman sit up all night baking wedding cake layers, mixing icing, making cheese straws, minted pecans, and a dozen other things for a reception. She was very organized and always worked at her own pace. She preferred to work alone because she had her own way of doing things.

I'd told her I would help in any way I could but she declined as usual. About two days into baking for the big wedding, the stress and fatigue really took its toll on her. I went by her house; I don't remember ever seeing her so flustered and frustrated. I offered to help but she said she'd be okay; she knew I had things to do. I all but insisted but my Mama could be very stubborn. As I pulled out of the driveway, I cried most of the way home just because it hurt so bad to see her struggle. I knew she was in pain but was just too prideful to let me help. Both my parents were like that, they just didn't believe in asking for anything unless it was an emergency.

That same evening, about six o'clock, my phone rang. It was Mama; I could tell something was wrong by the way she said my name. She asked if I could please come and help her. I knew for her to pick up that phone and call me it must be bad. I got there and found her sitting at the kitchen table; she was trying to mix icing up. Now for those of you who've never mixed up icing for a wedding cake, let me tell you that it's very time consuming. It makes a horrible mess and the clean- up is equally as horrible. She said her hands were so tired. I tried to be funny, uplifting, and cheerful. I made a joke and told her I appreciated her waiting till I'd got my pajamas on. I said, "Lord we gonna be here all night." She laughed and told me she had plenty of coffee and an extra cake layer.

I suggested she work on cake squares while I worked on the mixing; she started icing the sheet cakes. Bless her heart, a few minutes later I looked over and she was crying. "Oh no, what's wrong?" I asked. She looked at me so pitiful, wiped her eyes and said, "I can't squeeze the icing bags anymore." My heart broke in half with those words. It was all I could do to fight the tears back, but I did. Again, I tried to joke with her because even though she had such a serious side, she liked to cut up too. I just picked up the phone, called Linda and said 911; she was there in five minutes. Thank God for my cousin Linda through the years. I have no idea what we would've done without her many times. She was like a daughter to my Parents; they loved her and many times she went out of her way to do something for them. She didn't mind; her help came from a loving and giving heart. She was always like an older sister to me; after Mama was gone she became more of a mother.

From that point on Mama's health declined at a rapid pace. I no longer called her first thing in the morning because she'd begun to sleep in a little later. By this time, I'd already had my NDE. We'd talked a little about it here and there. She began to talk to me more about taking care of Daddy when she was gone; I just couldn't bear to even hear it. I would tell her of course that she was going to be around for a long time. She'd just smile at me and nod her head. One morning she said that she'd had the strangest thing to happen to her during the night. She woke up to see little marble sized balls of light in her room just hovering over the bed. I told her the angels loved her; they were helping her to get better. I knew that wasn't the reason but I wanted to be uplifting.

Over the next few weeks I opened up and told her everything about my NDE and what it had meant to me in my life. We talked about how none of us should be afraid of passing on because it was as natural as being born. A couple of months after that conversation, I pulled in her driveway to find her sitting under the carport. That was her favorite place to sit; she was talking to my youngest son. One of my sons usually went by when Daddy called and needed help. He'd been up on the roof with the blower. I heard the lawn mower. Daddy was in the front yard cutting grass. It seemed like a normal day for them, for all of us.

I'd told her we'd clean the blinds and do the windows. I wanted to help with some stuff around the house that day. Daddy kept up with the general cleaning but it always bothered Mama because she couldn't do the deep cleaning anymore. She said daddy didn't know how to do that. We talked for a minute and for the first time ever, I noticed an incredible calmness about her that day. She didn't say much which was unusual; she was smiling and listening intently to us talking. I still remember that peaceful look on her face. It was a beautiful look and I remarked how pretty she was. Mama was a pretty woman; matter of fact she was chosen for the Miss South Carolina competition when she was seventeen. Her Daddy wouldn't hear of it though because of the swimsuit competition. He said it wasn't appropriate.

She pulled out the Peebles sale paper from her pocket. She showed my son that the pullover he'd been wanting was on sale. She told him he ought to ride up there and get it because the sale would end that day. She insisted I go to; we were gone about 30 minutes or so. When we got back she was lying dead in the front seat of her Lincoln. I'll never forget that day as long as I live. It was one of the darkest times of my life for us to find her like that; we still choke up just talking about it. Nobody but the Good Lord in Heaven could possibly know how bad it affected us. Even though I knew in my heart her suffering had ended, I was so selfish in wishing that it wasn't her time to go. The two years of being really close to her before her death means the world to me; I wouldn't take a million dollars for it.

A few weeks later, Linda and I were cleaning out Mama's desk. We came across a sealed envelope with my name on it. When I opened it up, I found a letter that Mama had wrote to me. I read it over and over again, crying a flood of tears; it was evident she knew she was dying. It's taken me nine years to write this book, and for the longest time I contemplated even sharing the letter with you. But, I know in my heart Mama would want me too; I still miss her so …

Dear Donna Kaye,

As I write this letter I know my time left is short. As you all know, my health has gone down so much. When I retired years ago, my dream was for your daddy and me to travel. He did so much traveling when he was in service, but I never got the chance to go many places in my life. I was always busy working, helping to pay the bills. I took care of your daddy all those years when he was sick. So unfortunately, we never got the chance to fulfill my dreams because of my health problems.

I've known since I had my stroke earlier this year (2009) that I would not be long for this world. Oh, I've held on as best I could but am to the point when I lay down my head every night to sleep, I wonder if I will even wake up to see another morning on this earth. I remember when I first told you that I saw those little lights floating around in my bedroom.

I was afraid you would think I was crazy. You understood and told me not to worry; it was just my guardian angels protecting me.

You told me of things that happened to you. It made me feel better to know I was not alone. When it happened again, you told me I had guardian angels around looking out for me. You said I should not be afraid. I believed you and it made me feel better. You talked to me more about your near death experience and what had happened. I wanted to hear more about it for it brought me so much comfort.

I want you to know that you were always a good daughter. I always felt bad that you never had the childhood you should have had. You had to grow up way too soon. We were always in and out of doctor's offices with daddy and Lord knows we knew the emergency rooms of Greenville and Anderson hospitals well. I knew it was no life for a child but it was all we had and it was a tough life for all of us.

I always knew you were different. Even as a small child you were so caring of others and what they needed. Many times you asked me why daddy had to suffer the way he did or why others had to suffer. You were such a precious little baby. We waited seven years for you to come along and never thought we would ever become parents. But God saw different and blessed us with you. Unfortunately, when you first came to us my nerves were bad; it was hard for me to be the mother I had always planned to be. But I did get better and even though I had a hard time showing it, I loved you with all my heart and soul.

I'm writing this letter to you because sometimes it's just easier to put something on paper than to say it in words. I know you will be sad when I'm gone and probably mad I didn't tell you I knew I was going soon. But don't be sad for me. I have had a glimpse of Heaven, or as you say Home, and it is far more beautiful than any place I could have ever visited here.

Last night I had a dream but it wasn't a dream. It was very real and I know in my heart that you of all people will believe and understand what I am telling you. I walked with Mama, Daddy, and family who have gone on many years before. I even met my Brother that passed away before any of us were ever born; it was just like you told me and more. I used to be so afraid of dying. I was afraid my whole life because I thought of it as the end of everything and I was scared. But I'm not afraid anymore because I know what waits for me. I'm ready whenever it's my time. I've seen that it is much like where we live now only without all the bad stuff, and much more beautiful.

I saw buildings, parks, beautiful flowers of every kind, and many friends and family members who will welcome me with open arms. There would have been a time I would have been scared to death, but no more. My mind is sharp but my body is worn out. I've been sick for so long now and I know it won't be much longer. I wish I could bring myself to tell you about my vision before I go but if I do, you're not going to want to let go. You just can't stop living life to mother me.

You told me some time back that one day you would write your story for everyone to read. I don't really remember saying anything to you that day except, "well that's good." I'm sorry for that; I want you to write your story and tell everyone what you know and what I know. Tell others about what we have been blessed enough to see and experience. I want to help them to believe and know that it is real. Don't ever think about giving up on your dream because I will be here with you to help, I promise.

If you've found this letter then I will have already gone on. I don't want you to be sad for me; I will be in a wonderful place. I'm waiting for the day when the rest of you come back home. Your daddy will have a hard time by himself, so you and Guerry take good care of him. Everyone always thought because of his health problems that he would have gone on years ago. I never would have thought we'd have been blessed enough to be married fifty four years. It's not easy on the one left behind when you've been married that long.

I love you with all my heart and I know you will take care of everyone. I want the Grandchildren and Great Grandchildren to know I love them. I can promise you that I will find a way to let you all know that I am okay. You told me that our loved ones give us signs so I want you to look for mine.

Remember in your heart that I have always loved you and always will; I will always be with you all. I know that one day we will be together again. That is why I am not afraid anymore. Love everybody, love each other, be good to each other, and be good to yourself too.

With all my love,
"Mama"

I don't even have the words to explain what that letter has meant to me through the years. I bet I've read it dozens of times and each time I feel her near me. Mama kept her word; she's sent me many signs to let me know she's with me and she's okay. These little signs just reassure me that one day I'll see her again.

I never really understood what she went through or how she felt until now but I am so grateful she loved me and my children the way she did.

I appreciate now so much what I couldn't have possibly appreciated then. I could never thank her enough for the way she sacrificed for many years to take care of others. Not only did she work and take care of me when I was small but she cared tirelessly for Daddy when he was sick. She always made sure things were done right; we had what we needed. After my divorce, she and Daddy helped me with my three children more than I could have ever hoped for. They did it out of love for those kids and for me. I think now how there must have been many days when she was so tired after work. She could have done anything she wanted, but she chose to be the greatest Grandmother ever. She juggled her schedule outside of working around her greatest loves. To this day if you ask my children about my Mama, they have many fond stories of her and the love she had for them.

Chapter Ten

Message on the Interstate

Many times the other side will use any means available to grab your attention; they can be very sly and creative. If your angels, guides, deceased loved ones, and friends have a message to relay to you they'll be very persistent. It doesn't matter where I am or what I'm doing because time and space to them is different. I can be in a doctor's office, the grocery store, at a funeral, the hospital, or just talking with someone. I've been in restaurants, the nail salon, driving down the interstate, at someone's home, the movie theater, and anywhere you can possibly think of. I even had one fellow to approach me in a Starbucks. Bless that little guy's heart behind the counter; he'll probably never be the same. Anyway, I think you get the main idea here. Basically, if they know they can communicate with you, they'll do their best to make it happen.

Most of the time it works the same way for every one of us as far as communication goes. We all have the ability to interact with the Other Side for it is our true home, the place we come from. The problem is, some people are just not as open to the spirit world as others. Sometimes people are born with a natural talent for doing so; it's like they never forgot how to use it. Others have to experience something like near death, for theirs to emerge.

Still others work hard at developing their skills; they have that gut feeling there is just more to life than what we see or hear.

There are naysayers who would have you believe the spirit world is evil, deceitful, or whatever colorful adjective you'd like to label it with. I don't doubt there are some negative spirits because there are; I've witnessed the antics of some of them myself. There is also a rule I live by and one I tell people to always consider. I pray every day like many of you do, sometimes several times a day. In my prayers, I always ask God to please keep my heart pure and to help me only to focus on good intentions. I also ask God to only send the departed souls to me that need help so that I may be a mediator only for good. Keep in mind, if you do everything out of love, with a grateful heart full of thanksgiving, and a desire to help others, then you never have to worry about the negative aspect of the Other Side. You just say a prayer, give it to God, and let the universe take care of it.

I consider myself one of the many blessed individuals who've had the opportunity to learn from our dearly departed; they're great teachers, if only you'll give them the chance. Once you begin learning what it's really like over there and how they're just waiting to help you, you'll come to appreciate them and their guidance even more. It's been my experience through the years that there are three main factors that hinder the communication between our world and theirs. Number one is to not really believe the spirit world can communicate at all. I like to call it the old "Well I kind of sort of believe it but I just don't know," syndrome. Even though I witnessed many miracles growing up, I'll be the first to admit I never knew the REAL power of the Other Side until after my NDE.

Next on the list is our conditioning; we've been led to believe that once our loved ones die, that's it. We're taught that once they're gone, they cross over and there's no more sadness. We picture them sitting up there on the fluffy clouds playing a harp all day while listening to the angelic choirs sing. Does any of this sound familiar? Last but not least, we're so distraught over the fact our loved ones are no longer with us, that it actually hinders them coming through to help. Think of it as a block because that's just what it is and it's in the way.

I've talked with many people and it always works the same. If you believe in the Other Side and you're open to receiving helpful messages, hints, and clues, then they'll find a way to make it happen. If you're not, then it's definitely harder for them to give you signs and signals. I'm not saying it can't happen I'm just saying it might take a loooong time. I've also seen cases in which after a certain time period of grieving, a person still can't seem to let go. They just can't get over the fact that their loved one is no longer here for them to see and communicate with. I've witnessed a lot of different ways the Other Side works from the time I was a child and especially after my Near Death Experience.

I can't help but recall a lady who came to me in my local Dollar General one evening. Yes, sometimes for me just shopping at Dollar General can be quite an experience. I saw her looking around as to make sure no one would hear her talking. About 75% of the people who approach me say the same thing, "I just don't want anyone to think I'm crazy." By the way, I got permission to tell this story but I still won't give her name. She said she'd heard I was the lady who talks to dead people. I told her I preferred to say I communicate with our departed loved ones because we really don't die. She told me about losing her son; it had been five years since his passing. I could honestly feel her pain, she was pitiful. She just couldn't accept the fact that he was gone, therefore she grieved nonstop. It had affected her to the point she'd gone on medication and had to quit her job.

I ask if she would consider coming to my house for a visit. Now, I've never charged one penny for talking with someone about their departed loved ones. I work, so I feel it's something I can do to provide some comfort for those who need it. Who knows, after I retire I may hang out a shingle that says Carolina Medium; better yet I'll just run a contest and let you all choose the name. Anyway, when I do this, it takes a lot of my energy.

Matter of fact, there are days I'm totally drained so I have to be careful as to how many people I talk with in a short time period.

This poor soul came by the next day. After making ourselves a cup of coffee, we did the most important thing; we prayed. I asked Jesus to comfort her through sending a message or messages via her departed son. It didn't take long for the messages to start flowing. Basically, her son told her that he loved her and always will; he thanked her for being such a wonderful mother. Of course the tears flowed from both of us as she listened intently. But the last message he had for her, was to somehow find a way to please let go so he could get on with his work. He said he works with young people on the Other Side whose lives have been cut short by their actions. He indicated he was a counselor and he had much to do.

I watched her face almost instantly regain some youth. She began to laugh and smile; she told me that sounded just like him. She said for many years she thought that was what he would choose to do for his profession. She had encouraged him to get the training he needed for that career. Then, he just never went through with it, she said. Before she left, she told me it was time to honor his memory by getting her life back together. Last I heard, she was going back to school and taking classes for a new job; she was doing fine.

Now I'll be the first to say that we all grieve in a different way; no two people are the same. Sometimes we grieve for a short time; other times we grieve for extended periods. With that being said, I would never ever try to tell somehow how long their grieving period should be. But, I can tell you this. Our loved ones never want us to grieve to the point that it affects our health, our jobs, and especially to the point we have to go on medication. If you could talk with your loved ones here and now, they would tell you to take heart because they are right where they are supposed to be, depending on the life they lived here. They're doing work on the other side according to that, sometimes accomplishing things there that they couldn't while here.

Now with that being said, let's move on. If I had a dollar for every time someone tells me that what they're about to say might sound strange I could take us all to Disney World. I can assure you with every fiber of my being that nothing, and I do mean nothing, sounds strange to me anymore although certain instances do stand out. I remember one time in particular that was a first for me as to the lengths a husband would go to in bringing a message to his wife. I don't mind saying it left me with my heart pounding and my pulse racing. It advanced me one step closer to having nerves of steel and realizing just how powerful the Other Side is.

One afternoon while traveling through Knoxville Tennessee, I noticed a lady coming off of an exit ramp trying to merge into traffic. Bless her heart, it was busy. For those of you who do a lot of traveling you know how hard it is sometimes just to get back on the highway. The gross amount of cars and trucks on the road these days is unbelievable. I gave my signal to move over in order to let her in without success. Finally, after slowing down and speeding up several times, she managed to merge and move over into the middle lane. After that, she slowed down once again and held traffic up; horns were blowing left and right. After a couple of minutes she regained her speed and everything seemed fine until she began changing lanes. Have you ever just had the feeling that someone is frazzled or maybe they got their driver's license at Big Lots? Well that's the feeling I got when I saw her and witnessed her driving skills.

As I moved beside her, I noticed an elderly gentleman I assumed was her husband sitting in the passenger seat. Now let me make one thing perfectly clear; I'm learning more and more with each passing day never ever to assume anything. In all honesty, you'd think as many times as I've had spiritual encounters now, and the many people I've helped, that I would never assume anything at all. I guess one could say I'm just a glutton for punishment or maybe I just enjoy a challenge. In the back seat was a boxer bulldog staring out the window. I have a special fondness for boxers because my Dad raised them when I was small. When I passed her car I got the surprise, or should I say scare, of my life when I noticed the man looking straight at me covered in blood. I nearly jumped out of my seat as a rush of adrenaline ran through me. It's not every day you have someone pass you that looks like they were an extra in the Walking Dead series.

Once again, she changed lanes moving over in front of me. Then I saw her give a signal to turn into the upcoming rest area. In all fairness, I didn't know exactly what to think. All I know is I had an intense energy go through my body and felt like I needed to do something. I contemplated the idea that her husband had been in some type of horrible accident and she was trying to get help. Maybe she wasn't thinking straight; had she called 911? Why wasn't he in the back of an ambulance being rushed to the ER? How could he even be sitting there in that seat? My mind was flooded with questions and emotions.

In a split second I made the decision to signal and exit into the rest area. "Why am I doing this? I'm no doctor or nurse, so why am I bothering to stop? I'm sure she'll find the help she needs. There's bound to be tons of people there that could help." My stomach had butterflies and my legs felt like jelly as I pulled in and got out. I was surprised to see her standing with the door open, stretching her arms up high in the air and yawning. You would've thought her to be on a cross country journey, trying to regain circulation once again.

I hurried over, noticing the man still in the car and asked if I could help them in any way. I believe it went something like this, "Mam, can I help you and your husband in any way, is there something I can do for you?" I noticed her looking toward the car then she lowered her arms while giving me a puzzled stare. She added a crooked grin but didn't say anything. Again, I pointed to the passenger side of the car and asked if I could be of help. By this time I was about frantic, yep, full blown lunatic mode. I just couldn't get over her being so casual, uncaring, and nonchalant about the whole situation.

"Honey, I'm not sure what you're talking about," she said. "Your husband, he needs help, can I call someone for you?" She gave me the same look again with one eyebrow raised and by this time, I just knew I was the main actor in an episode of the twilight zone. Did someone forget to send me the memo on this? Why was she just standing there? Why wasn't she calling for help? Good grief, was she in shock or something? None of it made any sense at all. Lord, was I involved in one of the worst nightmares I'd ever been in or what? I started to pinch myself to see if I was even awake. Then she threw the zinger at me by saying that her husband had been gone almost two years.

I tried without complete success to compose myself. That was after I picked my jaw up off the ground. I watched the man get out of the car without opening the door. He was accompanied by the dog with a red collar and leash. He looked straight at me and gave a little grin and a wink while the dog just sat on her hind legs panting. "I know you did NOT do what I think you did," I thought while staring his way. I knew at that very moment he was in spirit form; he'd appeared to me with blood covering him because he had a message for her and wanted to get my attention. Now I've learned through the years when I see spirits that look more real, like we are here, it's because they recently crossed over or they are in the process of crossing over. By recently, it could be just a few years in earthly time. When they look more faded, like what I would say a ghost looks like, it's because they've been gone for some time. I can assure you that it takes a while to figure all this out but when you do, it definitely makes sense.

I must have looked like a mental case standing there in the middle of the rest stop parking area. How in the world would I figure out a way to tell this lady that her husband had a message for her? Lord, how in the world was I ever going to convince this woman that her deceased husband had been riding with her just to get my attention? "It better be a good message," I thought to myself. Believe me, sometimes it's not easy, each situation is different; you never know how people will react. I've had some to break down and cry while others laughed their heads off. I've had people tell me they knew their loved one had always been there. I've had some to simply look at me like I just escaped from the mental institution while passing the time by waiting on the men in white coats in a van to show up. But through it all, I've learned most folks are very receptive to messages from their loved ones. They might not be at first but it doesn't take them long to warm up.

I've also found that it's better just to spit it out, go with the flow of sort, so that's usually what I do and exactly what I did. "Mam, I'm sure this is going to sound crazy," and again if I had that dollar for every time I've made that statement; I'm sure by now you see a pattern emerging. "I'm not sure what your religious beliefs are but I can see people who are no longer with us. I can see those who have already left this world and your deceased husband is here with you." This is usually the point where they either breakdown, walk away, or stare at me like I've just flown in on a flying saucer. This time, I was met with a get out of here are you serious stare; she proceeded to ask if I could describe the man I was seeing.

"Yes mam, he's wearing a blue and white checked shirt with navy slacks. His left forearm has an anchor tattooed on it. He has on black boots, and a monogrammed belt buckle with the initials JJ on it. He's also wearing a silver and black bolo tie. He's quite bald with a red strawberry birthmark about the size of a half dollar on the left side of his head." Keep in mind he was pointing out these things to me. Sometimes they do that I guess, to help them be recognized. At least that seems like a fair assumption; there I go assuming again.

"Yep, that's him," she said, "that's him to a tee." She told me she'd always felt him around her. The whole family thought she was crazy so she never talked about it much. She said he'd come to her in her mind many times and in her dreams. I learned there was an accident with his tractor. It rolled over on him and he was crushed. He was covered in blood and already gone by the time she got there; she always felt guilty about not finding him sooner. "He would never carry his cell phone with him much. I begged and pleaded with that man. I always asked him what he'd do, or how he'd call in case of an accident. He never paid me any mind at all; just went throughout his whole life like a cat with nine lives."

Then she chuckled and said she wasn't surprised at all that he was riding along with her. "I admit I'm not the best driver in the world," she said. "Never have been sweetie, just never was my cup of tea. He always drove wherever we went. He said I just didn't have any sense about me out on the road. What few times I did drive us somewhere, which wasn't much, he fussed from the time we left till the time we got back. One time he broke his leg and couldn't drive for over six weeks. Lord I thought the man was going to have a spell before he got that cast off. He said that six weeks aged him twenty years."

"Was his name Jimmy?" I asked. "Sure was, James H. Johnson; always went by Jimmy." "Do you mind my asking if you two had a boxer bulldog?" "We sure did, the old girls been gone about five years now, she was his pride and joy." She spoke of him bringing that little boxer pup home years ago; she said it was the sweetest thing. He'd given it to her for a Valentine's gift. "I asked him why he would bring me home a dog instead of jewelry or candy or flowers." She said he just smiled and told her that little rascal looked like she needed a home. "Yep, it was supposed to be my dog but it took to Jimmy and never left his side on the farm for almost sixteen years. She was a true and faithful companion."

I asked if she had family in Connecticut; she confirmed she did. Then I relayed his message of urging her to consider selling everything. He felt a move to Connecticut to be closer to the family would be best for her. She gave me a little grin and said, "Young lady, now let me just tell you something right now." At this point I thought uh oh, I may have hit on a nerve. I know you might find it hard to believe, but I have a few times. "My son has been trying for a year to get me to do just that but I've been telling him no. Jimmy and I put everything we had into that place: blood, sweat, and tears. I've honestly wanted to sell it but

I thought he'd be upset." She said she knew it was too much for her to handle anymore.

I assured her it was his wish for her to sell and live with her son and his family so that she would be cared for. All of a sudden, a gorgeous 57 Chevy appeared to the side like it was in a barn covered up. It was candy apple red and shined like the new moon. It looked like it had just come off the showroom floor. I was able to see that Jimmy and his son had worked on it together; sort of a father son project but something had gone wrong. I had a sinking feeling in the pit of my stomach there were hard feelings involved.

Jimmy indicated to me he wanted his youngest son to have it. When I relayed the message to her, she looked really confused. She confided that her husband and son had a falling out several years before he passed away. Her husband vowed never to speak to him again. She wondered why he changed his mind. Her son always felt bad about what happened; he'd tried to make things right. "My husband was just too stubborn to say he was sorry too," she said. She always felt bad for their son because her husband would never truly forgive him. She said she tried talking to him many times about it but with no success.

"Lord a mercy that man was stubborn. He was a good man, a wonderful husband and provider, but stubborn as the day is long. His whole family was like that," she said. She told me that many times their lives could have been easier if only he'd put aside his pride and give in a little. She said he could never keep a true friend because everything had to always be his way or no way. "Jimmy always treated people, including the kids, like he was in some kind of competition with them. Many times I had to be the mediator between him and someone else," she said. "Sort of the peacemaker I suppose and believe me, it got old after a few years. But I loved him and tried to be a good wife."

"In all honesty, I was always embarrassed at how he sometimes treated folks. He only had a handful of people he ever really liked, never would give folks much of a chance and I was right the opposite. I love everybody," she said. "He always had that everyone is out to get me mentality, if you know what I mean. I thought he was crazy a great portion of the time but I could never tell him that cause it would set him off like a firecracker."

It was clear to me at this point that although they'd had a good marriage, there were many troubling and unresolved issues as well. I began to realize just why he'd gone to so much trouble. He felt he couldn't move on in the spirit world until he settled his family business. I find that a lot; our loved ones can't move on until they make things right. That's why it's so important to forgive while we're here. We need to make amends for the wrongs we think we've done because it does hold us back.

One of the most profound things the spirit world has shared with me the past few years, and on numerous occasions, is the importance of making peace before we exit this life. When we do shed our bodies and cross over, we learn first and foremost that all the choices we made while here, have consequences whether good or bad. These consequences are not just for self but for everyone involved with any situation.

For example: Jimmy showed me the scene where he and his son had the big falling out. He couldn't see it while here because he was just too pig headed and stubborn. His son was only trying to be closer to him but he took it as competition. He got so mad that he never forgave him for it. What hurt the most is what Jimmy experienced when he crossed over. He saw that because of his actions, rage, and unforgiveness, his son never went on to pursue his lifetime dreams of being a basketball coach. During his life review, he saw where many young people could have been coached and helped by him. Because of his actions and shutting his son out, he never got the chance. This is how it happens folks.

I told her that when we go home to the spirit world, or the Other Side, we do what is called a life review. It's much like the premiere of a movie but it's a movie about our life from birth till the day we pass. When we pass on, there is nothing but pure love there. One of the things we experience for review is situations in which we did things we probably shouldn't have done. We witness things we said to hurt others, times we could have helped but didn't. The number one thing we see, is how those we've hurt by word or deed were affected. We experience the hurt we inflicted on that person or persons, so we will know how they felt. But, the feeling is so much more intense. I can assure you that no one gets by with anything. I think I hear the whistle of the Karma train. We judge ourselves based on how we've lived our lives and treated people; we learn from the experiences we had while here. Again, please remember that Karma is not meant for punishment, only to learn lessons.

I ended our conversation by assuring her how much he loved her and always would. He said she was the best wife, mate, and friend. He was so sorry he didn't listen to her more. He then confirmed that he would always be with her forever. The last thing he told me to tell her was, "we don't die, we only go home, and next time I hope to get it right." She hugged me tight and thanked me for helping her. As I walked away, I looked back to see him and his faithful companion one last time. With a nod of the head and a heartfelt thank you, they were gone. I left that day with the most peaceful feeling that in some small way, I'd helped to maybe make someone's life here and on the Other Side a little easier.

Chapter Eleven

Jan

Death, as most of us know it, can be a very strange bird as my mama used to say. Growing up we'd often times sit up with our departed loved ones. It was just a natural thing. You never tried to shield your children from it because it was life. Folks in my area, well a great majority of them, believe one way. That way is when you die, you'd better have a good relationship with God; if not you're in trouble.

After my mother in law's husband passed away, she was absolutely distraught. He was the love of her life. Even though she tried her best, she never really got over him being gone. Whenever we were home, which was about every other week, Jan would come and stay with us. Bless her heart, she was just so lonely. Because Randy was a few years younger than her, his passing away at the age of fifty-three from a heart attack left her with many questions. It's been my experience the past few years, that even though we're brought up not to question, we still do. We can't help but wonder; that's the human side. How could our loved ones be taken from us, especially when it's sudden?

I've talked to many people on numerous occasions who have loved ones they feel crossed on over too soon. Fact is there's no way for us to know for sure if it was in God's timing, or something we did to cut our life short a bit. The Other Side tells me our bodies are designed to live for one hundred and twenty years. Unfortunately, because of all the bad foods we have today and many other factors, years are taken away from us.

Let's say you've been a heavy drinker for twenty five years. You find out one day you have Cirrhosis of the Liver. Not long after the diagnosis you pass away. You'll always have that family member standing there, or a person that will say, "bless his heart, it was just his time to go." Well, the Other Side tells me there are things we do that can and will cut our time short here. The opposite side of that is we live a clean life, try and stay healthy, do for others, get plenty of sleep, etc. No matter what we do, it's just our time. That's why I say we really never know; only God knows all the answers.

I had a lady argue with a spirit one day about this very thing. Bless her heart she'd lost her brother to a drug overdose. He had a message for her because he knew she wasn't over his death. He came through telling her not to feel bad because it was his fault. He said he could've lived a long good life had he not abused his body. She told me to tell him not to worry that it wasn't the drugs; it was just his time to go. He let her know right quick it wasn't and he was in some serious therapy on the Other Side because of the way he lived his life. He said he went through what the Other Side calls "cocooning." I've been told that means wrapped in the arms of the angels and care workers for a certain period of time.

Jan was there for me during many deaths of family members, including my Mom and Dad. She was a very intelligent lady, one who didn't mind thinking outside the box on lots of subjects. After my near death experience, she would ask me questions from time to time about certain things, or aspects of religion. After the passing of her husband we talked all the time about the spiritual side. I assure you, there are many differences between being religious and being spiritual. This led to many discussions between the two of us about our present life and the afterlife.

Not long ago our family experienced a tragedy, one I would never have expected to happen. As we all know, life is but a fleeting moment. It's imperative we enjoy our time while here. It's important we love each other and try our best just to be happy; treat each other right. Honestly, I've learned that we just never know when, or if, we'll have that chance again. I'm sure that many of you can relate to this. We live and learn as they say. Hopefully if we live long enough, it will finally sink in to our thick heads.

I'm actually sitting here writing this chapter in the window seat of my mother in law's hospice room. It overlooks a peaceful little lake in Jacksonville, FL. It's a comfortable padded seat; the sun is shining in during late afternoon. It's almost mesmerizing just to feel the warmth on my face. Only a few days before, Jan was walking around my sister in law's house laughing, cutting up, and having the time of her life. She finally seemed happy, but all that came to a tragic end when she took a bad fall and hit her head.

Now I sit here and listen; she struggles to breathe, yet at times she looks so peaceful just lying there. To my right, I catch a glimmer of the glistening water in the sun. I feel the rays on my face through the blinds. I'm barefoot and comfortable; the energy in the room is peaceful and low key. My husband has the most beautiful Irish and Scottish music playing softly for her. I can't help but think when it's my time to go, I hope my final setting is this restful.

Jan had experienced some health problems, but still managed at 81 years of age to be somewhat independent. When she reached the point of becoming more forgetful, we made the decision of moving her to live with my sister in law Diane and her husband. Guerry and I travel for a living, and although she'd not stayed with us recently, we felt she needed to be with someone full time. She was lonely; life became very overwhelming for her as it does for so many of us.

Her days before the accident left her with a sense of happiness and contentment. Times in which she enjoyed being able to laugh and reminisce with her daughter and family close by. It was such a blessing for both of them. About 3 hours before my sister in law called us, I developed one of the worst headaches I've ever had. I hardly ever get headaches but this time it was terrible. I continued to keep that headache throughout the next few days, almost non- stop until her passing. When I had my NDE, like so many others who've experienced that and come back, my talents began to emerge. When I say talents, I mean those gifts given to us by God to use while we are here.

One of mine is being highly empathic; sometimes it can be a blessing, other times not so much. The definition of an empath is "a person that is affected by other people's energies, whether positive or negative and has an innate ability to intuitively feel and perceive other's desires, wishes, thoughts, and moods." Being an empath is much more than being highly sensitive; it's not limited to emotions. I've found on my empathic walk, there have been times I've felt things so strongly it's made me physically sick; at least in the beginning it did. There were days I felt like I'd been hit by a boulder. Thankfully, I've learned to control it. I still feel these things, but less severe. I'm affected just enough to get my point across to someone, without it affecting me to that degree.

The fall caused her to develop a Subdural Hematoma. Because of being on blood thinners, surgery was not an option to relieve the pressure the first few days. By the time it was out of her system and possible, it was too late. She'd already had a stroke and her condition had deteriorated so much. In the first few days following the accident, when she could still communicate with us, she would say her head felt like it was going to explode. It didn't take me long to realize being near her was the source of my head hurting even more.

I'd experienced this with my dad as well on occasion when he would fall and hit his head, which he did often. It affected me in much the same way. One time when daddy fell, he hit his head so hard I thought I'd developed a case of Vertigo for a couple of days. I found during the time with Jan that my head constantly felt pressure, almost like it was a balloon being blown up with helium. In my experience as an empath, when this happens to me, it's only a fraction of the pain the other person is actually feeling; I can only imagine how horrible it was for her.

At first we all prayed the bleeding would simply stop on its own. The doctor said there was a fighting chance it could, but time would tell. We just knew, because of her being such a strong woman, she would pull through; we had no doubt it would be a long recovery. I still remember the phone call, throwing clothes in a bag, and driving all night to get to Jacksonville to be with her. At first, and this is very important to remember, when we got there she cried and said, "I don't want to die." I have no doubt she knew the seriousness of her condition. We hugged and cried with her; we assured her she was getting the best of care.

Minutes turned to hours and hours to days. When this happened, as many of us have experienced, we began to notice her slipping away from what we perceive as normal. Now I wholeheartedly believe in the power of prayer. Many people were praying for her and for us as a family; we felt all of them. I can honestly tell you that there was a supernatural presence around us as the days grew darker. That day came too soon and we knew in our hearts, it was just her time to go; she wasn't going to make it.

As I said earlier, she and I had extensive conversations through the years about death of the body and the afterlife of the soul. But no matter how much you've talked about it, you're never prepared; none of us want to die. As her condition steadily worsened, her whole outlook and demeanor changed. Late one night my sister in law, myself, and a cousin were sitting in her hospital room. We were talking to the nurse who was telling us some questions to ask the Dr. the next morning.

We thought she was in a deep sleep because of the medication, but she heard every word we'd said. Now most of the day she'd not spoken, she just slept a lot on and off. When she did wake up, it was as if she really wasn't there. The stroke had also impaired her speech some, so her voice was quite low when she did try and speak. All of a sudden, she just started talking to us like her normal self. We practically climbed up in the bed with her. As she was speaking, Joan began writing down her words. It was one of the most wonderful and heartfelt experiences I've ever been blessed enough to be a part of.

The power and energy in the room that night was so intense. It was filled with so much love, my body tingled all over. She began by saying, "You are all angels and I love you; your hands are so comforting to me." She talked as if going down a list of family members. We knew she was leaving parting messages for each of them; it was really quite remarkable. It was at that moment I began to notice her face change. She went from a not knowing and fear of the unknown look, to one of being so peaceful. She told us not to cry; she said, "The Angels are here with me now."

We sat there, emotions running in every direction, comforting her and each other, with tears flowing like waterfalls. My guide has said for years that tears are the waterfall of the soul. She told us she couldn't wait to be with Grandmother, Grandad, Randy, and Bobbie; all of which had been gone for years. Then she looked straight ahead and stared. With the most peaceful look on her face, she began talking as if she were giving a speech in front of her class. She said these words, "For every problem under the sun there is a solution or there is none. If there is one, try to find it, if there is none never mind it." She said this was her mantra. She was leaving us girls with her final lecture. After that she went to sleep for a while.

Now I know what some of you readers are thinking. I've heard similar things a hundred times from a hundred people, those who don't believe like we do in the afterlife. You're thinking, "Oh it's just the medication she was taking that made her do that." I do agree that sometimes medication makes us talk and act in strange ways. But, when you know someone and you've been with them in this type of situation, you know in your heart what they are seeing is very real.

The next morning, my husband and I were there with her. She woke up, raised her arm into the air and smiled. "There's mother,

I see mother," she said, "there's Grace, she's so nice; she's waiting for me." In conversation years before, I'd told her Grace was her guide. She'd not been able to remember that in months.

We sat on the side of the bed feeding her ice chips; she complained so pitifully of being thirsty. She couldn't have liquids because of the stroke. I began rubbing her face with a cool cloth. I could almost feel how soothing it was to her. All of a sudden, she began to talk to Guerry. If you've never had the opportunity to sit with a dying loved one, it can be one of the most heartfelt and moving experiences of a lifetime. It's such a blessing just to be with them when their time is near.

The dying can tell us so much if we'll only listen. As their time nears, the veil between our world and the world they return to grows thin. They see glimpses of just how beautiful and peaceful it is. They began to remember where they came from, so as to make their return journey home easier for them.

At this point tears were streaming down my face, flowing faster than I could grab tissues and blow my nose. She squeezed my hand and said, "My precious Donna, my angel, don't cry; don't cry my sweet Donna. Heaven is everything you said it would be and more." Then she pointed up and across the room and said, "I see Jesus, he's handsome; he's playing the harp for me, the music is so peaceful." Now I can tell you this, when you hear your loved one say those words, if it doesn't stir your heart then nothing will.

At that point she smiled with such a perfect peace about her. "I'm dying, but I'm not afraid," she said. "I see where I'm going and it's a place like I've never seen before; Randy is waiting for me, I want to go." It was at that very moment, and I still get chills when I think about it, that her face began to glow. It was almost as if a bright light was shining through from somewhere in the room onto her. It was one of the most humbling experiences my husband and I have been blessed enough to have.

She stared off once again. "Donna, your Papa says he loves you." I assumed at this point she was talking about my Dad because my Children and Grandchildren called him Papa. I said, "aww, thank you; tell Daddy I miss and love him too." She turned her head and looked me square in the eyes. "No, YOUR Papa, he says you always loved the little ponies and riding, you always loved the horses." She told me he was taking care of my little Bitsy too. At that very minute, a chill ran up me. There was no way on earth she could have known that. My Papa passed away when I was only seventeen, twenty-five years before I ever knew Jan; we never spoke of him even one time. I had Bitsy from the time I was a year old. She always went with me to Papa and Nannies; she died a few months before Papa.

Papa was a strong influence on my life growing up. I often stayed with my Grandparents on their small farm; I was especially close to him. I followed right behind his steps everywhere he went, Mama would say. When I was only five, he and Daddy bought me my first pony. Many times, Papa would stand and lean on the pasture gate and watch me ride. He had the patience of Job and it hurt me terribly when he passed. It meant so much to receive that message from him.

It was that same afternoon that the hospital Chaplain came in and patted her on the shoulder. She told him that the angels were all around her and she felt peace; they were waiting on her. She talked on and on for a few minutes. I watched that man take his glasses off and rub his eyes. He told us that he always considered it an honor to stand at the foot of the dying and witness the many wonders they could tell us, if only we would listen.

On several different occasions before going to the Hospice House, she talked about the man who visited Daddy when he was dying, the angel. She and I talked about him many times and she loved to hear the story. She always said when it was her time to go, she hoped he would come and be near to her. She told me she prayed that Jesus would send the same angel to her that comforted Daddy. She asked me the day before she was moved if I would pray for God to send him. I'd love to share what happened with you; I think it would mean a lot to her.

Daddy fell out of bed on June 4th, 2014. He'd experienced memory loss for a couple of years, with the setting in of Dementia a few months before. Honestly, it took our whole family almost to care for him. Daddy was my buddy. We did the best we could to give back to him, he deserved that care. I promised Mama he'd never lack for anything and I was determined to keep that promise. My Daughter and her family actually moved in with us to help because we work out of town so much. I can't begin to count the times my Husband, Sons, and Son in Law picked him up off the floor or the ground after a fall. We had every test you could possibly think of run, in hopes of an answer as to why his legs would just give way on him while walking; he'd been living with this for years.

Keep in mind, after the angel visited him many years before, he was healed from all his kidney issues completely. He never had another kidney stone, and never once had bleeding from the kidney ever again. For many years he lived in peace from any major health problems. Several years after retirement, he began to have some heart issues, as well as a few other things. Over all he did pretty well on a daily basis. Then one day when he was in the yard working, his right leg just gave way and he fell. He was always able to get up on his own until his stroke. After that, he fell more and needed help getting up.

We did everything in our power to make the house more accessible for him. Although he did walk with a cane, he would never hear of using a walker. I can't begin to count the times one of the neighbors stopped and helped him up when no one was home. I can never thank each of them enough for their acts of kindness. Eventually, he became homebound due to loss of muscle in his legs. My nerves stayed on edge in fear that he would break something. He never did, but boy did he ever bruise himself. He would scrape his arms so bad, the skin literally hung off when he would fall.

That particular morning his fall was different though. We chose to call the rescue squad because we felt he needed to be seen.

After running some tests, we were told he'd had another stroke. I was so worried because he never fully recovered from the first one, so we knew it was bad. Bless his heart he hated hospitals. I guess as many times as he'd been in one, he just detested even hearing the word. We settled him in his room but over the next few days, his condition worsened. I always felt so bad because he spent his birthday in the hospital. After a week of being there, the doctor put in the order for rehab. He wanted to see if they could help him regain some of the strength in his legs. We thought the therapy would be great.

Daddy was only in the rehab section for a few weeks. He struggled just to do the exercises. He would say it hurt so bad to move his arms and legs the way they wanted him too. They were good to him but he just couldn't do it; I knew he'd given up. His poor old body was tired and worn out from all he'd been through. He'd been so ready to go for so many years. I can't begin to count the times he would tell someone who visited, that he just wished the Good Lord would take him on. It was one of the hardest things I've ever gone through in my life, just to watch him struggle.

We were all set to bring him home. I was in the process of ordering a hospital bed, while thoughts of how we'd now care for him raced through my mind. I knew it wouldn't be easy, but I also knew our family would work it out somehow. I visited with him before leaving on Friday, telling him I'd be gone for a few days for work. I assured him the family would be checking in every day. I promised him when I got back, he was coming home. I remember him smiling and pointing to the red birds outside his window. When I looked, there were none to be found. I humored him by saying that they sure were beautiful; he was fine when I left. Half way through our trip I got a call saying he had taken a turn for the worse.

My Daughter left work; she called and confirmed that something was definitely not right. It's hard being so far away when your loved ones are sick or hurting; I got back two days later.

When I arrived, I found him lying in bed, looking straight ahead with a fixed stare. They did scans and confirmed he'd had another stroke. This time, the doctor said he would never recover from it. Over the next few days he got progressively worse to the point his eyes stayed shut. His breathing became even more labored, even with the oxygen; I knew his time was getting close.

I stayed with him almost constantly at this point. It was late one night; I was sitting next to him in a chair. I had Andy Griffith on the TV in the background because that was one of his favorite shows. It just seemed to add a little comfort. I was reminiscing about our lives together and how good he was to me growing up. Lord, I loved that man; he was the best Daddy and Papa in the world, or at least to me he was. All of a sudden, I got that all over tingle again; I began seeing little tiny, marble sized lights. It was as if they were coming out of his chest. I sat there mesmerized as I watched them hover over his body for a few seconds. I saw them band together and float away right through the ceiling. I must have sat there in shock for half the night, not knowing what to think.

As I drank my coffee the next morning, I felt guilty for even doing so. I knew how much Daddy loved his coffee in the morning. I thought about all the times I saw him come through with his cup headed to the TV; I knew I would never see him do that again. I listened as his breathing became even more labored. It was a horrible time for me; I cry as I type these words and to this day, I still can't talk about it without tearing up. Sometimes there are benefits to being an only child; other times, it's so difficult. When it all comes down to it, you're the only one that really knows what the feeling of losing a parent is like. Somehow I kept the thought in my mind that when Daddy left, I would feel like an orphan.

Across the hallway I could hear and see one of the nurses as she worked on the medicine cart. I was watching her, when all of a sudden I heard whistling. A man stuck his head in the door and asked if he could come in. I had no idea who he was but I told him yes, please do. He was wearing Khaki pants, dress loafers, and a red pull over polo shirt. I remember this because he looked like he'd just stepped out of a men's fashion show. I'd say he was in his middle forties with thick wavy brown hair. I distinctly smelled Old Spice; Daddy always wore that too.

He asked me how I was doing; I smiled and told him okay I guess. He sat down for a minute and looked over at Daddy. "You know, your Dad has always been a good man, an humble man," he said. "He's certainly kept the faith through the years and been a fine example to others." I agreed that yes he was. He told me he remembered how happy my parents were when they found out about me because my mother couldn't have any children. He said they tried everything to no avail but they sure were happy when I came along.

Now by this time I'm sitting there asking myself, "Who is this guy anyway and how does he know about all of that?" I'm thinking just how does he know Daddy and especially things that only a few people ever knew? It just didn't make any sense. I was about to ask him his name, when he got up and stepped over beside Daddy's bed. He put his hand on Daddy's forehead, closed his eyes, and prayed silently for a minute or so. After he finished praying, he turned to me and said, "You know he's not in there don't you? He's already gone sweetie; that's just the old worn out shell of a body holding on."

I was so stunned at his words I couldn't think of a thing to say; I just sat there. But somehow, what he told me was so comforting. I knew at that moment what I saw the night before was his soul leaving his body. I knew what was left, was just the body hanging on, not wanting to let go. His voice, words, and smile made me feel like everything would be okay; I knew Daddy would be fine. Then he patted me on the shoulder and said, "You'll be okay, it just takes time; he'll always be with you." I watched him walk through the door and as he turned to go, he gave me a little wink; then I heard his fading whistles as he left.

As I tried to process what had happened, I got up and went to the door; I asked the nurse who that man was. She looked at me sort of puzzled and asked, "What man sweetie?" I told her the man with the khaki pants and the red shirt. I asked if he was the Chaplain. She looked around and said, "ain't been nobody here but me sugar; I never saw no one go into or out of Mr. Davenport's room but you." I told her what happened and we both just looked at each other. I have no doubt he was an angel; I believe he was making his rounds bringing comfort to those who needed him that day. Daddy officially passed away early the next morning when that poor old body finally turned loose.

Now that you know the story, I'll finish up with this. When Jan was in Hospice and her time was growing near, my Husband, Brother in Law, and myself, were walking down the hall. We were heading home for a bit to get something to eat. All of a sudden, I saw this man coming down the hall; he was just a whistling. He was wearing khaki pants, had on a red pull over shirt, had thick wavy brown hair, and smiled like he had so much love for everybody; I almost fell over. He walked right by me, winked, and gave me the biggest smile. I stopped and said, "Wait a minute, that's the guy who came to visit Daddy, that's him." When I turned around to see him, he was gone. My Husband and Brother in Law both saw him and the scent of Old Spice lingered in the hall. My Mother in Law passed away a couple of days later.

Chapter Twelve

Random Thoughts

For the past few years, I've had the privilege of asking countless questions of the Other Side. Most are about life in general; some I've received an answer, still others I have not. I've learned first and foremost, if I don't get an answer, it's one of two reasons. Either my guides don't know, or it's not meant for us to know. Another important point is that our guides never, ever interfere with free choice and free will. If I ask for advice or help on something, they will often offer suggestions but that's as far as it goes. I'm told because of free choice and free will, they are not allowed to make decisions for us or to say you should or shouldn't do something. It works this way for everyone; it's like a Universal Rule.

A lady told me a very sad story a few years ago. She talked about her brother. He got mixed up with drugs as a young man and went on a shooting spree; several people were injured and one killed. When it came time for his trial, the mother of the young woman who was shot was allowed to speak. She asked one question of this young man, "Why on earth would you ever do such a thing?" He replied by saying, "the voices in my head told me too."

Now with that being said, I can assure you no spiritual helper on the Other Side would ever tell him or anyone else to do something bad, much less such a horrendous act. If he was hearing voices, it was most likely a negative entity he allowed in because of something he shouldn't have been doing to his body. Another reason could have been he was strung out on drugs. That's just my opinion and it's only an opinion from past years of communication with the Other Side; it happens folks. When we live outside of God and God's principles, bad things often occur. When we choose to live a life that brings about evil thoughts, decisions, and acts, it can only lead to the worst of consequences. Not only for that particular person, but many times those who are innocent as well.

The Other Side never ceases to amaze me once you become spiritually open to their help. As I sit here typing and drinking my coffee, I was mumbling to myself, thinking about the right way to word a certain thought. I constantly ask for guidance in writing so my words may help those who need it. All of a sudden, a book fell from off the shelf; just tumbled right to the floor (this has happened to me on numerous occasions). I walked over, picked it up, and read the bold print words on the open page, "Guides Help You-They Don't Do Your Work For You." Wow! Now you see why I am constantly amazed?

The spiritual helpers on the Other Side are always ready to lend a hand. Don't ever worry about asking for too much help because they just don't see it that way. God created them to help; all you need do is call on them. One day I had a lady say to me, "I don't believe in that; I believe that God is the one and only way. You should only pray to God and not to the others." Good grief, who said anything about praying to your angels and guides? I mean really; I never once said we need to pray to the angels and guides for help.

I have one source I pray to and that is God, Jesus, Yahweh, the Creator; you know where I'm coming from. I talk to Him daily, without hesitation I pour out my heart. That's just a routine with me as it is with many of you. Now I often refer to God as He, but I do wholeheartedly believe in the female side of God; it's just easier to say He because of my upbringing. Thankfully, God is egoless so the reference doesn't matter. With that being said, God made the angels, God made every one of us, God made the helpers on the Other Side. Why did He make these helpers? To help us of course; that's why we call upon them when we're in need. We're not worshipping or idolizing them, we're asking for help. Please don't be so narrow –minded, thinking that God has such a fragile ego, He will be offended if we ask his blessed creations for help. I assure you that God is way beyond those negative humanistic feelings.

An acquaintance expressed her concern just the other day about asking for help. She was afraid of allowing some evil entity to come through. I assure you that negative, or lower level beings, are very real. I've stated this before. Personally, I don't deal with them because I choose to live a life of love and helping others, so they don't mess with me. I pray, asking God to only let me commune with those helpers that are good. I seek guidance daily; I pray for a discerning nature about me.

Your angels and guides are here for you and those around you. They will always be gentle and loving, considerate of those you care about. They will never ever make any type of suggestion that will cause you to do harm, or bring harm to anyone. If you encounter anything else, you'd better run as fast as you can, because you just haven't grounded yourself enough to keep them off your team. Honestly folks, it's not that difficult. People make it out to be so complicated and it's not. It's another Universal Rule that says if you pray and ask for help and guidance and you ask that only good sources come through, I like to call it God Approved Sources, that's what you're going to get. If you ever get guidance that is negative, threatening, frightening, unloving, or discouraging in any way, then it's not God Approved. Do everything out of love, with the Fruits of the Spirit mentality. Never settle for less than the God Approved seal. The Other Side tells me this is learning to listen to our higher self; again that's for another book.

There are high vibration guides and entities or helpers, and low vibration entities; we want to only associate with the high vibration helpers. The Other Side knows how hard it is here on Earth; they know our daily struggles. The low vibration pranksters will play upon you by filling your head full of crazy stuff. They'll tell you what you should be doing and how you should do it; if you don't, they'll try and make you feel worthless. The high vibration guides only recognize the good in you. They see you as a beautiful person designed by the God Source; you are precious to them. They only want the best for you and are here to help you in any way they can; they just don't tell you what to do. They make suggestions by giving you that gentle little nudge; it's called that gut feeling. It's there for a reason, so use it.

I had a lady come and talk with me a few months ago; she wanted to get some salve. I told her I was talking with one of my friends but she was welcome to come on by. My friend and I were discussing angels, guides, etc. and how much her life has been so positively impacted by these dear beings. She explained how she asked for guidance on a daily basis. I've watched this dear soul go from no job, being on six types of medication, and having panic attacks, to having a great job, no medication, and no panic attacks at all; sound familiar? After my friend left, the lady picking up the salve gave me a look like you wouldn't believe.

I felt she had something to say but couldn't exactly find the words. So you know me, we talked for a few minutes and I prodded a little; I asked if anything was bothering her. Boy did she let me have it; yep I stepped right in to that one I tell you. She accused me of fraternizing with demons and anything and everything in between. I couldn't help but get a little tickled as I thought, "Lord, if she only knew, ha ha." Seriously, sometimes I could have so much fun but I didn't, although I wanted to.

So I posed this question to her, "what would be your definition of me fraternizing with demons?" She became very flustered, turned six shades of red, and began to mumble how if you worshipped anyone but God, you're doing the devil's work. I really could've had a blast with that one, but I didn't. Aren't you proud? At this point, I felt the need for a huge cup of coffee. I poured the both of us a cup and we talked for two hours. First of all, I pointed out that there is one Creator, the main one and that is who I answer to. I included Jesus in that because I'm a huge fan of His. Then I explained again, for the gazillioneth time, how I never said anything about praying, worshiping, or anything else of that nature to the angels, guides, or any other spiritual helper. Lord, my head is spinning again just typing this.

At this point Red Cloud intervened to relay this message to her. When I asked if she would mind if Red Cloud spoke, she almost spit her coffee out all over me. After she got over the initial shock, she hesitantly agreed. Red Cloud explained first, that God created everything; we have no doubt about that at all. Now this is the part I love; it's great. He explained how there are people who are religious and people who are spiritual. He never takes away from being religious, although he highly recommends giving spirituality a try. When those of us who are spiritually enlightened, and by that I mean, ones who seek the truth, encounter those who are not, we are constantly asked about consorting with demons by the dear souls who don't know any better. Was that enough of a run on sentence? I've honestly tried to keep those to a minimum.

Anyway, low level vibrational entities don't want any of us to know the truth; they want us kept in the dark. They don't want you to know that God is love; they don't want you to know how fantastic the Other Side is. They don't want you to know about past lives or learning lessons. They don't want you to know that we have spiritual helpers around us every day, like angels and guides who are always with us. They want you to have a spirit of fear; they thrive on it. And here is the million dollar question? Are you ready for it? How do they accomplish this? By telling you if you call upon your spiritual helpers that it's wrong and you are consorting with demons. I've even had people shake their finger at me and say, "Omg! You must be evil because you're psychic." Who said I'm psychic, I just talk to the Other Side and those dearly departed loved ones who've gone on. I'm taught that when you really and truly receive God into your heart and life, you'll automatically want to know all aspects of God and where you came from. Believe me folks, the only way to do this is to shed some of the old narrow minded ways and open your heart to what God is really all about. He's the one and only, He wants you to know the truth. Once you do this, you will never again view our world the same way.

I've had many years with my guides now and hundreds of conversations about thousands of different subjects. At first I tried writing everything down, but after some time, I found I just couldn't keep up. There's just not enough time and book space to share everything. But, I'd love to share with you some of the things I've asked about and the answers I've been given. Some answers you may perceive as pure common sense; other may seem off the wall. You'll notice that some may seem a little incomplete as well. I hope you enjoy this section!

*   *   *

I've always been so intrigued with the pyramids. When I asked about them, I was told that the pyramids of old were built with the intention of being used as energy portals. Man worked alongside beings, not from our world, to erect these great structures. It was a time of peace between our world and others.

When I asked about the Pineal Gland I was told that the Human Pineal Gland is the seed of consciousness. If properly cared for, the body is cared for. In earthly words, if it is cared for, everything else falls right into place.

Next, we have the human body. I was told it is made of pure energy and electricity. They stress that it would serve each of us well to begin our day by stepping out into nature, into the sunshine for a few moments for by doing this, we absorb the sun. I'm told that if possible, it would serve us well to stand barefoot during this time with our feet touching the Earth for grounding.

I asked if they could say a little more about the human body. I was told it performs at maximum capacity for which it was designed when alkaline. They say the body often becomes acidic, not alkaline. It performs best with optimal rest; it was designed in that fashion.

I've always had the feeling there were other races, this is a direct quote, "Surely you would never think your race as being exclusive to the universe? There are many universes that make up creation. Your human mind may have a difficult time perceiving this. There have always been beings, entities, everywhere beginning with Father Yahweh."

I asked if they could elaborate a little more on other planets and the beings that inhabit them. I was told there are many planets. Some of the planets are inhabited; some are desolate. Some of the desolate planets were once inhabited. Through some force of nature, or by the hand of the beings that lived there, the planets became unstable. In some cases, the beings perished. In other cases, the beings were relocated to other planets of similar composition. Some are like us in their body make up and composition; others are nothing like us.

I asked if Earth is at the end of her time, this is the answer I received. "We must be cautious as to how we answer this so as not to confuse you. Your Earth is in the cycle of a great awakening. There is an awareness being brought about once again. This cycle has happened before, many times. Humans are beginning to wake up and realize how they have treated the Earth. Women are realizing they have been suppressed for far too long. Humans are beginning to return to their roots, the roots that grow strong and deep in the earth. Once again, mankind is demonstrating unselfish acts, proving that the human race can love and appreciate the qualities of the Creator."

When I asked for more on the Great Awakening, this is the answer I received. "We would say that mankind is recalling what has been forgotten for so long. It would serve you well to seek less religion and more spirituality. Some people worship the songs they sing in a religious ceremony. Others seek and feel the Creator whom the song is about. Some worry about the clothes they wear to their religious service and time spent preparing those garments. Others contemplate if they have spent their time in enough prayer and talking with God. Some worry about the words of the sermon of the one who speaks to you. Others seek spending enough time in prayer, asking God to fill their hearts with "His" sermon. Your people spend so much time and preparation for a religious ceremony. Because of this, they have no time left to listen for God's communication with them in proper manner. Those of you who realize this and choose to concentrate your efforts toward God instead of a ceremony, will be the ones who advance at a faster rate. We will give you an example of what we mean.

We know of a lady who has been a member of the same church for over twenty-five of your earth years. She teaches a class; she plays the piano for others to have music. She spends many hours each week preparing for her lesson and several hours playing the piano in practice. Each is a commendable act, very admirable; her efforts lead to good works. She helps many people by doing this, souls have been blessed on many occasions. She performs this same routine each week and has, for twenty plus years. Many times she has read the verse in your Bible that states this, "For whosoever will save his life shall lose it; and whosoever shall lose his life for my sake shall find it- Matthew 16:25."

She has always understood this verse to mean that she should give up things in life and be committed to her church, faithful to attend activities. As we said, while her works are commendable, she has never really understood what the verse actually means because of miscommunication. Then one day she has a revelation, an awakening in which she realizes the true meaning of this verse.

She sheds her earthly ways in decision that it is time for her to grow even closer to God. In doing this, she announces she will no longer be teaching her Sunday School class because she has no time to prepare. Instead of taking the time in preparation of the lesson each week, she is volunteering her spare days at a homeless shelter preparing food for those less fortunate. She is instead sitting by the bedside of a dying body at a hospice facility reading words of comfort, praying with and for that body. She is instead sitting alone in her garden in deep prayer to God, asking how she can be of service best to others. She now spends a great portion in time alone and silence talking to God, listening to what God has to say. She decides she will go out on the streets and tell anyone who will listen about the love of God and what God wants for them. She decides she will go into the prisons and speak with those who reside there, telling them of God's love.

Now we would ask you this question. Of the two life scenarios of the woman we gave you, and keep in mind that both are commendable, which sounds more of how the Master Jesus would react? Would he be caged up in a sanctuary each and every week, performing the same routine in hopes that someone would come to know the love of His Father God? Or would he go out and help to make it happen? Would he take to the streets and share with anyone who will lend a listening ear? The real meaning of the verse we shared is this: "For whosoever will save his life shall lose it," means, if you are willing to give up worldly things, your habits, your routines, and have faith enough to go out and be a true witness for God, then you will better understand God and how God works. "And whosoever will lose his life for my sake shall find it," means that when you do these things, it brings about an awareness, an awakening in your soul. With that awakening you begin to realize just who God is and the power you possess in helping others as it is given to you by God. With all of this realization comes a closer walk with God that leads you to the Kingdom of Heaven.

Would we tell you at this point to leave your church, to give up your duties, to give up everything you know and think you love? No, we would not do that, for it is wrong on our part and not permitted. But in everything there has to be balance. If you choose to observe these religious ceremonies each and every week, then that is your free choice and free will to do so. It is evident that those of you who do, would greatly benefit by not frowning upon those who choose a different system. For some that choose a different, non secular path, they are just as close as you, if not closer to the Creator. You who choose this weekly routine are in your own way close to God and that is once again commendable. Those that choose the route of spirituality over religion, are sometimes the ones who truly understand what life is all about and how it should be lived. Many a person has gained a close and personal relationship with God sitting in her own home, walking in the woods, or working in the garden. God is everywhere, not just in the confines of an elaborate, expensive building.

We talked extensively about Karma and their answer may surprise you a little. Here is what a member of the Divine Council told me. "Your definition of Karma and our meaning, may vary somewhat. Karma is the opportunity for learning and growth; it is not meant to be for punishment or associated with it in any way. You say, Karma will get him for what he did. We say, because of what he did, he will experience the pain and hurt associated with his actions, therefore he will learn valuable lessons. It may not happen in this same lifetime, but it will happen we assure you."

Then I asked about what could be done if we feel we've wronged someone. Is it possible to make amends for our wrong actions?" Rachel answered this one. "Yes there is, this is a very valid question. It would be wise to seek the person you have wronged if possible, explaining that you are remorseful for your actions. Next, you may satisfy karmic debt by practicing good deeds such as helping those less fortunate, etc. It would serve you well to satisfy as much karmic debt as possible before returning home. The reason for this would be to make right, acts that have been committed against others. In doing this, Karmic debt is lessened."

Next, I ask about insight on prayer, our bodies, and healing; just general advice on this. "Yes, we are glad you have asked this of us, for we are always eager to help address these subjects. It would serve you well to practice both prayer and meditation. Prayer is the act of talking to the Creator Yahweh, while the practice of meditation is listening to what the Creator Yahweh has to say. No, it will not necessarily be audible in the form of words, although this has happened on occasion, it will be more of a still small voice we have talked of; the knowing what is right and wrong.

Colors bring about healing; it would serve you well to study this. We suggest becoming familiar, really familiar with red, orange, blue, green, yellow, violet/purple, indigo, pink, white, magenta, turquoise, brown, grey, black, gold, silver, and copper healing qualities. We could write an entire chapter on copper healing qualities. These are the prominent healing colors of your world.

Music is also healing, as many of you already know. It would serve your body and soul well to find what tone resonates with you, each individual is different. What resonates with one, may not necessarily work for another. The key to music and healing therapy is what truly resonates with your soul.

We have stated before the importance of love as opposed to begrudgement, hate, and jealousy. When you live daily with these negative qualities, there will become a manifest of disease in the body. There is no choice but to happen. It starts out small then festers like a sore. When you love and practice love for your fellowman with love in your heart, the body stays much healthier. We have stated before that your bodies are designed to operate much longer than the life span you are currently accustomed to.

It would serve you well to shed your love of material wealth and possessions. Doing this may gain a closer relationship to the Creator Yahweh through living a life of service to others. One cannot possibly know this concept until they have had nothing. What a humbling experience to lose those things you have worked for. In losing your valued possessions, you truly find yourself, which leads you to find your true nature which is the heart of the soul.

It would serve you well also to study the effects of an alkaline body versus an acidic body. Disease resides within an acidic body.

The body is also designed for optimal rest. It is very necessary to achieve the rest your body needs for optimal health. Some of you require more rest than others. You must do what is best for your body and system; there is no shame in rest.

You would do well to practice sleeping in a dark room, void of any light. The dark room helps the body with the making of the melatonin process which is associated with rest. It is very important to the healthy body process.

It would serve you well to distill your drinking water, storing in glass or crockery. Copper is excellent as well, we highly recommend the use of copper, but one must have knowledge of this element. If you have access to natural spring water, then by all means utilize it. There is also much to be said for the experience of fasting. It would serve you well to study the effects."

Next I asked for another fascinating aspect about the Earth. I got many answers on this subject but this one stood out with me. "Your Earth is filled with time portals. They do exist because the past, present, and future all cross simultaneously. One example is the Bermuda Triangle where past, present, and future meet. Many have passed through this channel into another dimension. This one in particular is very strong, it contains much energy. The magnificent creature you term as Bigfoot, Yeti, Abominable Snowman, Sasquatch, it is not native to your planet but to your world. It comes to your planet through portals. It respects your planet and enjoys the vegetation you currently have. We will be astounded if the creature is ever caught here for it is elusive and very intelligent. It is also a compassionate creature as well."

Next, I asked if there was any other important information they had to share with us. Wow!!! Did I ever open a can of worms. Here in detail are some of the most fascinating subjects they talked about. I could go on forever but the book can't.

"Your entire book of Revelation refers to the activation of the Solar Force in the spine. It would serve you well to study the Chakras and their meanings. If your body feels heavy and weighted down, your life force energy is not working properly. We see a great number of people burdened now with the diagnosis of Chronic Fatigue Syndrome. This may be corrected by restoring the body's energy system. There are many laymen and practitioners familiar with the Chakras and life force energy. You would do well to seek them out so that you may learn from their expertise.

For those of you who experience what is termed Fibromyalgia, you must work on the healing of the Root Chakra. This is where the problem lies. Because it vibrates at the lowest frequency, it is easy to become out of sync if not cared for. It would serve you well to study the disorders associated with the Root Chakra and set your intentions on restoration.

As we have stated time and again, there are many paths to the Source, or as you say God. Some of you call it levels or realms, there are many. You may envision the Other Side as being paved with streets of gold, with the angel choirs singing and structures made of precious gemstones. That level, we assure you, exists. But, you must understand there are many levels. The one which was just described takes many lifetimes and many lessons learned to reach that level. Some of those who have achieved this level are Christ Jesus (who was the only begotten son of God), Mother Mary (mother of the world), Paul the Venetian, Lady Nada, Melchizedek, Gautama Buddha, and Krishna; we could go on forever. This level is meant for the soul who has learned everything it can possibly learn.

In the beginning of time, Father Yahweh made the Divine Council to rule with He and Mother God; they longed for a family. You may say that God is beyond that feeling. We say man was created in their image and man is much about family unity. Father Yahweh bestowed some of his abilities and knowing to the council and they were pleased. The time then came for man to be created and Father Yahweh made the decision to grant some of his abilities, as well as gifts, to humankind. This was done because He longed for the unity and ruling of all creations together. Father Yahweh would for all eternity be the all knowing and all seeing, with his creations being the caretakers for him. Sadly, a percentage of the council did not appreciate the knowing and gifts bestowed upon humankind and rebelled. As we have already stated, those who rebelled caused much hardship upon humankind. With this came the battle of good and evil. Father Yahweh made it known that his creations, all of them, would contain the God Particle. The rebellious ones made it their mission to make man look bad. This is where your Biblical account of the fallen angels and Lucifer began and sin entered into the picture.

You may think you know the scriptures, but most of you do not. In order to know the true teachings and how existence came about, as well as Father Yahweh's teachings, you must go back to the Hebrew Scriptures. The truth lies within these sacred texts. Many of your modern religious traditions did not even originate with God. They came about after the Biblical Era. Many of them were born out of fear and idol worshipping. We would encourage you to do your homework. We could write a whole book on this subject alone.

We must recognize that within the spiritual world, there is rank. Father Yahweh has always been, is now at present, and will always be at the very top. All creations fall under Father Yahweh. The councils created and appointed by Father Yahweh help mankind in the daily struggles of life but Father Yahweh has the final say. We bid you go in love and peace."

In closing out this chapter I find that so many people are conflicted by their religious teachings. Each soul has a specific purpose here. I've found through talking with hundreds over the years and through many different belief systems that even though our beliefs may differ somewhat, we all have one thing in common. We're all searching for meaning in our lives.

If I've learned anything at all through my studies, it's that we can't judge people who don't think or believe as we do. We all have to follow our paths and beliefs; it's not up to us to point fingers. For me, I'm constantly searching for knowledge and wisdom, for a higher truth so to speak. The number one question people ask me is, "What happens when we die?" We don't die folks, we just step through another door and carry on as usual.

Printed in the United States
By Bookmasters